The Insurance Talent Magnet

If you build it, they will come.

By Justin Goodman

Table of Contents

INTRODUCTION

One of the most iconic lines in the history of sports cinema also happens to be one of the most misquoted. Even movie fans who haven't seen Kevin Costner's *Field of Dreams* are likely to know the phrase, "If you build it, they will come." But the actual line is slightly different: "If you build it, *he* will come." Kevin Costner's character, Ray, is a struggling farmer, and he builds a baseball diamond in the middle of a cornfield...because he heard a voice in his head. The he in the line is Ray's favorite, long-dead baseball player, Shoeless Joe Jackson of the infamous Black Sox scandal. Creating that baseball diamond becomes his obsession, but later in the movie, after seeing the spirits of the Black Sox playing in his field, Ray must consider selling the farm to avoid foreclosure. Terrence Mann, played by James Earl Jones, encourages him:

> People will come, Ray. They'll come to Iowa for reasons they can't even fathom. They'll turn up on your driveway, not knowing for sure why they are doing it...They'll pass over the money without even thinking about it. For it is money they have and peace they lack.

This scene is the essence of this book. It is true that if you build it, they will come. While money is important, peace—a sense of belonging and purpose—are driving factors for most people. Much like Ray, you need to build it, not just to survive, but thrive. You need to build your talent magnet.

In the talent-driven economy, attracting talent is one of the most critical aspects agencies large and small must tackle to survive. But companies are learning that this isn't enough. It isn't sufficient to just hire good people. You must have a detailed action plan to onboard, train, and retain them. Employees now see themselves as the center of their economy. They can shop for employment opportunities, much like consumers shop for products or services. To be successful, agencies must fully understand how employees want to be recruited (and by whom), and that begins with knowing what attracts employees and what draws them into that process of researching and discovering the opportunities available to them.

What Is a Talent Magnet?

Your agency's survival depends on building a powerful talent magnet. One that will help you attract and retain the best of the best and set you apart from your competition. Talent magnets attract more qualified candidates than the company has job openings. As a result, you'll have the opportunity to cherry-pick talent while others are scrambling to find B-players.

It's no secret that the top-performing organizations have best-in-class talent magnets. Think of a few of today's great organizations and their branding. The company's branding creates a desire to work there and attracts experienced talent. Branding, building a reputation, recruiting, and retaining top talent all continue to feed the loop—brand to attract, recruit, retain, modify, and brand.

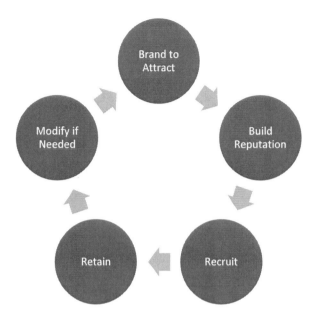

Take Google, for example. Google is and has been a respected brand and has built a reputation as a top employer. They are well known for being a great place to work and a destination that supports a long-term career path. They attract top talent from around the world, including over 3.3 million job applicants in 2019 alone. Of those, only 0.2% were hired. Google doesn't need to compromise when choosing talent. They get the best and brightest by attraction.

So how do you make the leap in the insurance space?

But I'm getting ahead of myself. Before we define a talent magnet, we need to clearly define talent. We have all had that one employee whom we want to clone. We might call them A-players, unicorns, or other names, but they all tend to have a few things in common that land them in the "top talent" department.

Now, you may be wondering what top agency talent looks like. In general, consider the following traits:

- **Being coachable.** You need talent that is open to learning, practicing, receiving feedback, and evolving with the organization.

- **Thinking independently.** You need to recruit those that can follow directions but overcome more complex challenges to support the agency's goals on their own.

- **Having empathy.** Insurance protects people, their property, and their businesses. If a prospective employee starts every sentence with "I," that may give you a glimpse at how empathetic they are. Despite the advances in technology, we are still a people business, and our team members seek to understand our client's issues and the impact those have on them personally.

- **Being results oriented.** Look for those who commit to deadlines, handle pressure, and are driven to meet the agency's objectives and, more importantly, those of the client.

- **Being a great communicator.** As humans, we communicate with words and emotions. A good communicator can work through difficult situations and conversations even when emotions run high. Telling people what they need to hear in a way they can receive it is essential. Don't mistake the gift of gab for being a good communicator.

- **Being career vs. job focused.** Think about whether

you're recruiting someone who wants to build a career within your agency or someone who just wants a paycheck.

- **Buying into the vision.** When you discuss your agency goals, does the prospective employee see how they fit into those plans? Do they understand the vision in both the short and long term? Do they have ideas for how to help achieve that vision? Will they buy into that vision completely, even when they disagree with an aspect of the game plan?

- **Possessing the technical skills.** Technical skills are essential, and finding those who have them is becoming more and more difficult in our industry. We must start thinking differently about this. Rather than looking for someone with years of experience and the ability to leverage a certain agency management system, you should focus on computer literacy, writing capability, and the ability to utilize emerging technology. If they can do this, they can be trained in the rest.

- **Having the necessary aptitude.** Smart people with critical thinking skills are an absolute must given the complexity of the industry marketplace and resulting policy forms.

- **Being a personality fit for the role.** Certain personality traits are more likely to yield successful results in certain positions within a company. For example, a service-minded person might be able to cross-sell some accounts but likely would be unsuccessful in a straight production role. The reverse holds true as well.

We all know that the agency side of our business has three general career paths. The first two ultimately might grow into the third one:

- **Account Managers.** They handle all the servicing needs of our clients and are the agency's backbone. They possess empathy, strong communication skills, attention to detail, and excellent time management skills.

- **Producers.** Persuasive and possessing great communication skills, these employees have the drive to win, aided by a healthy ego.

- **Management.** Ultimately, account managers may find themselves leading service teams or growing into an operations lead. Producers also pivot into this role as well. However, agencies must ensure that the skills to lead are at the core of the role. Historically, I have found that top account managers and top producers are frequently mistaken for top leaders.

To attract individuals possessing the skill in each respective track, a strong talent magnet is essential. So, let's break it down in more detail. Simplified, a magnet is an object with a strong attractive force. Think about that person who oozes charisma. Imagine being at an insurance industry event and encountering someone you're drawn to or notice across the room and hope they make their way over to you. There is some unseen force that gets ahold of you. Those individuals attract others like them or who want to be like them. People are drawn to them, and those people then attract others. The same goes for organizations. If you have a strong pulling force, you can "magnetize" the people you bring in, who will attract others to your agency in turn.

When employees embody your organization's characteristics and culture, they are drawn to it and its success. They then attract others like themselves. Employees should want to align themselves with agency leadership and work to achieve your agency's mission. When they do, they become an integral part of the magnet. Your organization's magnetism rubs off, and as a result, they become magnetized. When they are, the power of your talent magnet increases significantly.

When you have a strong pulling force and your employees and organization are aligned, you create an environment where people want to work. In this setting, employees are of higher quality and are more productive. That's just good business.

Let's go back to Google. Do you remember the first time you heard stories about their culture? They have snacks, dry cleaning, laundry service, and on-site doctors. Google employees get daily catered lunch and other benefits, such as fifteen weeks of paid parental leave for new fathers and mothers. Oh yeah, and you can bring your dog to work! A large population views Google as *the* place to work, but what makes it so attractive? Why do the brightest minds in tech flock to this California-based company? What makes it a talent magnet?

Google goes beyond just perks and benefits to help its employees succeed. In the book, *How Google Works*, Page, Brin, and Schmidt describe a culture of creativity and innovation. Employees can form groups around any concept they choose. These groups aren't assigned projects or goals but work together toward a common goal with no set structure or endpoint, which encourages a purpose beyond self-advancement. Employees are given time to work on side projects that could contribute to Google's greater good. For example, when an employee noticed that Google's security system wasn't as secure as it should be after one too many lost phones, he created an Android Device Manager tool. This tool allowed them to locate and ring their misplaced phone from any computer or tablet—thus saving Googlers worldwide from lost phones.

Google invests heavily in its employees' creativity, curiosity, and desire to innovate. On top of allowing free time to work on their projects, Google also provides many workshops and seminars taught by some of Silicon Valley's most talented techies.

Taking care of employees is part of Google's culture. Beyond having an amazing product, they're successful because they have happy, productive employees who want to stay for the long haul. Of course, we don't all have the capital to provide perks at this level. But we can do better than we have been and leverage creativity and flexibility to bridge the gap.

That is the purpose of this book—to teach you how to build a best-in-class talent magnet. The concept is simple, but the follow-through is often difficult. For example, eating healthy, working out, showing up on time, and budgeting are not overly complex concepts, yet somehow, we either never execute or can only maintain momentum for a short period of time. Unfortunately, yo-yo commitment will not generate a powerful talent magnet.

So where do we begin?

This book will be split into two parts. The first will help you understand the landscape on which you'll be building your talent magnet. You can't build anything without doing a survey first, right? So, the best way to start is to understand where our industry has been, where we are now, and where it's going. The second part of this book is about your specific agency and how you can build a talent magnet by creating an ideal workplace that matches your culture and vision, keeps the right employees longer, and attracts more people to your agency (and to insurance in general).

Now, let's dive into the first portion of this book, where we'll discover how we even got to this point. Yes, it's a history lesson, but before you doze off, you need to realize there is a war—and it's come to your front yard. If you haven't read *The Art of War*, add it to your reading list. You're at war, even if you didn't know it yet.

CHAPTER 1:
THE TALENT WAR

In the midst of chaos, there is also opportunity.

—Sun-Tzu, The Art of War

We often lose sight of the big picture as time goes on. We live day to day, week to week, month to month. We are so focused on the quarterly new business goals, client renewals, or the implementation of the latest Insurtech, that we miss what's going on around us. Most agency owners wear multiple hats, so carving out time for forward-thinking business plans often gets pushed aside until year-end. And if business planning takes place, we're usually focused on cutting expenses, increasing revenue, or implementing tools to be more efficient.

Eventually, we catch a glimpse of our staffing issues. Most of us are understaffed, but we never really make a strategic plan to confront the issue. Instead, we just have our staff take on the additional workload. We turn to recruiters for established account managers. Or, as a last resort, post a job opening for a new-to-industry hire to train. Then, more than likely, they move on to another agency or industry a few years later.

Agencies aren't just fighting to keep their existing talent; they're fighting to attract seasoned professionals and new talent entering the industry. The problem is nationwide, and it isn't going away. In fact, statistics show it's getting worse by the month. In their February 2020 survey, Manpower reported that 69% of employers struggle to fill positions. That's up from 14% in 2010. By 2030, the talent shortage could be eighty-five million, according to the global consulting firm Korn Ferry. You'll fight this battle for years to come, so you might as well lean into it. With ever-increasing demand and limited supply in the labor market, it has never been more critical to adapt, build, and strengthen your talent magnet.

Specifically, the demand for quality professionals within the insurance industry has never been greater, and these professionals control the marketplace right now. So, agencies have moved from merely playing the "talent game" to pure, unrestricted warfare. The industry is no longer experiencing a labor shortage in which we can woo talent with the offer of a simple 10% comp increase. Not only are the competitive compensation offers dwarfing what they used to be two to three years ago, but they're coming with a whole host of other benefits too. Our industry is in crisis, and your agency is fighting a talent war.

The competition will use any and all resources to acquire talent, leveraging every tool at their disposal. Forbes recently reported on the escalating talent war and tactics. At issue are the noncompete clauses, which are enforceable in some states but not in others. In states that bar noncompete clauses, agencies put highly restrictive non-piracy agreements in place. Despite that, large agencies are willing to poach talent from competing brokerages and pay for the legal defense to get away with it. Many small agencies can't afford the cost of a prolonged legal battle, so they end up settling for pennies on the dollar or not pursuing legal action at all.

So, what's behind this all-out warfare?

First, the industry is watching older workers retire. According to the US Bureau of Labor Statistics, over four hundred thousand workers will retire from the insurance sector over the next several years. Second, the industry continues to struggle with attracting younger talent. A survey conducted by the Institutes reported that eight out of ten Millennials didn't know about employment opportunities in the insurance industry. Further, Valen Analytics wrote that 44% of those surveyed didn't believe an insurance career would be interesting.

The talent deficit results in agencies offering their existing professionals insane amounts of money and flexibility to get them to jump ship and move from X agency to Y agency. Agencies used to focus on poaching producers. Now, they're also poaching entire account management teams.

Along those same lines, agency consolidation continues to increase—the big fish eating the little fish. This will continue because there's too much investment capital on the sidelines and not enough places to put it outside the stock market. New capital-gains laws are also fueling private equity firms to gobble up more agencies. As they continue to scale, they need more talent. Given their cash reserves, they can afford to pay a premium for average talent. As a result, smaller agencies will struggle to compete for even mediocre employees.

Further, the black swan event of COVID-19 has permanently changed workforce dynamics. With some employees not wanting to come back to the office, agencies will (and are) poaching talent from other states and allowing them to work remotely.

The Great Reshuffle

The Insurance Labor Market Study Q3 2021 Hiring Trends reported, "The industry is amid 'The Great Reshuffle' as professionals waiting to make moves earlier on in the pandemic are now exploring their options and reevaluating their place at their current employers." This reshuffle has made recruiting—especially at experienced levels—extremely competitive, and it seems most agencies are in the same boat. Of those surveyed, over 80% said they intended to hire in the next twelve months due to being short staffed or having plans for expansion.

In addition, according to the 2020 Agency Universe Study Management Summary, "The average age of principals with 20% or more ownership in their agencies is fifty-five years old, with 17% of those principals aged sixty-six or older." The industry's talent woes have a two-prong problem: retiring professionals creating talent gaps and a lack of interest from younger workers to fill them.

45% of insurance agencies report that children or family members will take over the business for those aging out or retiring. Another 30% say a partner or other principal will take over. Legacy agency ownership is predominant. But how do you fill the positions vacated by those moving up?

Later, I will discuss the issue with younger workers who are not interested in an insurance career. But for now, let's talk about the tactic used to fill the immediate gap.

You either poach or be poached. Larger agencies have an advantage with capital, but that doesn't mean smaller agencies can't compete. Not everyone wants to work for "big corporate." In fact, we can make a strong argument that a majority of workers prefer the smaller, family-run agency environment. So how do you compete to draw talent when you aren't flush with cash for big compensation packages? By the time you get to the end of this book, you'll be equipped to do just that.

The Bottom Line

The talent war will be fought over the course of decades. The changes to the dynamics within the industry and the labor force are only accelerating. From generational preferences to technology and the economy, you need to reconsider recruiting and retaining employees at scale. You need to build a forward-thinking talent magnet within an agency niche that will bring top talent to you. The key is strategic planning.

CHAPTER 2:
GENERATIONAL DIFFERENCES AND THEIR EDUCATION

Each new generation is reared by its predecessor; the latter must therefore improve to improve its successor. The movement is circular.

—Emile Durkheim

Each generation has different needs and preferences, and that's just the social aspect. You can't use a one-size-fits-all approach in the workplace. We need to learn the needs and preferences of each generation. To find engaging ways to attract and retain top talent that are specific to each generation. So, what does that look like?

Generation Alpha

You might want to pay attention here, as this is the most recent generation. This generation includes the workforce you haven't thought of yet. Alphas are born from 2013 to 2025. Mark McCrindle, the social researcher who coined the term as a "new start" after Gen Z, has a few predictions.

This group is theorized to be more racially diverse and have higher economic inequality. They are also the most technically savvy and materially endowed of any previous generation. Thus, it's believed that they will stay in education longer, delay entering the professional workforce, and live at home longer than any other generation. McCrindle argues that this generation's exposure to screens at a young age will result in shorter attention spans and the need for a more gamified education.

This youngest generation is also working through a "new normal" with the pandemic. Lockdowns, online learning, masks, and vaccination mandates all shape and shift their habits and characteristics. We have already begun to see reports of issues with interpersonal skills and socialization, not to mention the skyrocketing mental health issues that will take years to work through.

Are you preparing for this eventuality? In ten years, this group will be graduating from college (if that still exists in the same way) or directly entering the workforce. You're going to need a plan to reach out in their senior year of high school and provide them with educational opportunities and practical work experience. In short, provide training-specific life skills and provide an opportunity for them to meaningfully contribute to the agency. We'll cover how to do this later in the book.

Generation Z

Let's dive into Generation Z. This generation was born between 1997 and 2010 and is the youngest of the current workforce. They are known for their desire for speed and efficiency. They want work-life balance and prefer visual information over text. All this may be no surprise, considering they haven't known a life without handheld technology, the internet, social media, and the instant gratification that comes with it.

Gen Z values training more than any other generation. 36% of Gen Zers say it's the top factor when considering a new job, compared to only 20% of Gen Xers. Now, don't confuse training with education. While Gen Z values both, there has been some movement toward alternative learning styles. The traditional university degree-seeking path isn't always the route they take— especially if it requires them to take on student debt.

They want to be able to shape their learning. Therefore, Gen Z is more interested in alternatives like custom learning experiences. How-to videos on YouTube, Udemy courses, and TikTok channels have gotten a bad rap. Still, entire online communities are dedicated to learning new trades, side hustles, cooking, cleaning, and even forums on leadership and communication. These platforms succeed in engaging professional, educational, and social material whether we like it or not! Your agency needs to provide training opportunities that consider these alternative— and often preferred—learning styles.

Gen Z prefers mentoring programs over classroom instruction and may favor a blend of hybrid or remote work over a structured office setting. They also tend to be more purpose-driven and desire a clear career map from their employer. If you fail to provide a culture that supports their preferences, they will likely move to larger organizations, hoping for promotion and more autonomy.

Millennials

Millennials are next in line. This group was born between 1981 and 1996. They often get picked on for being a little over the top, or even narcissistic, if you ask a boomer (or self-absorbed if you ask Generation X). However, this is the largest generation aside from baby boomers. They have been studied more than any other group, so we have lots of data on them.

When surveyed, Millennials revealed that the top reasons for leaving a position were better compensation and benefits, opportunities for career advancement, and more challenging work or projects. These answers align with the fact that Millennials are more educated than previous generations but also have the most student debt.

They need compensation packages that enable them to pay their student loans and still have a high quality of life. The student debt issue is so concerning that 55% of Millennials think company compensation packages should include debt payoff assistance. Companies are listening, and to compete in attracting top talent, they are changing packages to include student debt payoffs, among other things.

This generation also likes remote work and flexible work schedules. They don't want to work nine to five. This can be problematic (in concept) in an agency environment, where customers demand quick response times. That said, technology allows access to communication by email, phone, and call forwarding, which might mitigate some issues.

Another difference is that 88% of Millennials surveyed preferred a collaborative work culture over a competitive one, according to Inc.com. This makes sense, considering this generation reportedly has higher anxiety levels and more perfectionistic tendencies. So those sales production bonuses and competitions for account rounding are probably not great motivators for the servicing side of our industry.

In that same report, "84% say that helping to make a positive difference in the world is more important than professional recognition." With that in mind, have you considered incentives or opportunities for volunteering or organized charitable events?

When it comes to leadership and mentoring, Millennials were primarily raised by Generation X (which we will discuss later). Children from Gen X often had both parents involved in the workforce and were frequently left to fend for themselves. So, Millennials often had helicopter parents who wanted to fix everything, schedule everything, and structure everything. Gen X parents overcompensated by telling their children they were special and could do or be anything. As a result, Millennials (through no fault of their own) entered the workforce with high expectations of how quickly they could get from point A to point Z. They also would prefer mentor-friend relationships to supervisor-employee ones.

It has fallen on employers to undo some of the damaging habits created by good intentions. A common growth area is conflict management. Millennials frequently view conflict as inherently negative and either engage with it from behind the safety of a computer screen or avoid it altogether. They need help and practice to change this perspective and tackle conflict positively in a face-to-face environment.

Finally, this individualistic group has seen the negative impact and perceived disloyalty of agencies due to lack of advancement. That has always been an issue in our space but is exacerbated by Millennials' need for accelerated timelines. Most agencies don't have a full corporate ladder. They have a rung on a corporate ladder, and it's hurting them. In fact, the typical tenure of new hires is less than eighteen months.

Millennials have no problem leaving an agency for a 10% raise and then coming back two years later for a 15% raise on top of that. The idea that employees must first move out and up before they can go anywhere in their current agency has become an unfortunate trend in our industry. Millennials fell victim to a dubious management strategy practiced by countless agencies: the companies would not provide a meaningful raise, opting instead to absorb the recruiting cost and efficiency loss associated with replacing an employee. It's pennywise and dollar dumb but pervasive among the couple thousand of our agency clients.

Before 2008, immediately following the economic collapse, Millennials also saw that large agencies that had furloughed or laid off workers ended up not rehiring for those positions. But agencies didn't do this without valid reasons. For example, as a construction-focused agency, we lost 50% of our commission revenue almost overnight after the 2008 crash. Given the economic uncertainty, most agencies found they could expect team members to pick up the slack and do more work out of fear of losing their job. Obviously, this was not my insurance agency's strategy. I think it paid dividends for our culture, especially when you consider that we emerged from the financial crisis several years later.

But at many other agencies, if you were a productive worker and didn't get laid off, you were rewarded with more work. There was no raise or promotion when profit margins increased after the economic recovery. Shareholder value and executive compensation increased, but we told many Millennials to be grateful and better manage their money. Remember the comment in the news? If you stop buying avocado toast and Starbucks, you can afford to buy a house. Needless to say, Millennials weren't amused, and the lack of loyalty and appreciation from employers has had a lasting impact.

Generation X

Now for the group that raised Millennials! Generation X was born between the mid-1960s and the mid-1980s. They are named "Generation X" because they are considered the "forgotten generation"—partly because they were left to fend for themselves. These are the latchkey kids formed from divorce and bad economic timing. Mothers made their way to the workforce en masse, and Gen Xers found ways to raise themselves.

The lack of supervision and adult presence, coupled with societal shifts in family dynamics and the recession of the '80s, resulted in a generation where one in five Gen Xers grew up in poverty. As they matured into young adults, Gen Xers were self-reliant. They found ways to attend college, where they navigated the technology boom with home computers and, eventually, the internet.

The conditions and changes Gen X worked through were the perfect recipe for breeding entrepreneurship. They'd been indoctrinated into self-reliance and problem-solving. This group is often characterized as skeptical of authority, adaptable, resilient, resourceful, and pragmatic. Take note, as this group is often more difficult to convince and encourage to join the collaborative thought process. Interestingly, this collaborative process is precisely what we need right now. However, this group was the first to implement agency management systems, a shift to paperless agencies, and regular email communication over fax or phone calls.

When asked their reasons for leaving a job, Gen Xers included looking for more challenging work, better compensation, and benefits with advancement opportunities. This group, unlike Millennials, is very interested in benefit packages. After all, they remember the struggles, recessions, stock bubbles, and the like. They want a cushion for when (not if) something goes wrong. They value 401k options with matching contributions and formal career path development. You may want to consider offering them tuition reimbursement to complete a college degree that may have been out of reach before.

This group hasn't been as mobile as younger generations, but they will leave. Gen Xers tend to be more loyal but will transition to other companies after seven to ten years or so. This is when they feel their career paths have stalled and they are just receiving cost-of-living increases in their pay. There must be a bigger performance-based carrot that addresses their financial security concerns.

Baby Boomers

Baby boomers are the group born between 1946 and 1964. They were the result of servicemen coming home after World War II. This population was the largest generation on record and influenced business and policy for years, from the civil rights movement to "aging in place" care today. This group was resourceful and learned to fix things themselves, from cars and washing machines to eyeglasses and shoes.

Boomers are often thought of as old, slow, and behind the times—but don't count them out yet. They grew up and evolved from black and white television to cell phones and FaceTime. They grew up with a sense of duty and the American Dream. Yet, they were also the generation of the sexual revolution, hippie culture, and protest. They value relationships and hard work. Boomers value a purposeful mission above all else. Therefore, your company's mission and vision statements are crucial for them. There is a reported 49% lower attrition rate in this group when the company has a purposeful mission.

In the workplace, this group values retirement plans and stability. They want a flexible work schedule to take care of their aging parents. This group "remembers when" tasks were people-centric and took longer. They didn't have email, fax machines, or cell phones. Paperwork was just that: paper. You filled out customer forms in triplicate with a pen or a typewriter while sitting in front of the customer.

Baby boomers started at the bottom and worked their way up. They went through comprehensive insurance training programs. They usually had a diversified work history, going from underwriting to claims to the agency side of the business. They then settled long term at a company once they completed the first few years of on-the-job training.

Much of what they did and had to learn was more comprehensive than what's required today. Many policy forms were manuscript in agencies, and a much more comprehensive understanding was needed to adequately protect the insured. They also had to really develop soft skills, as the first half of their careers required a tremendous amount of face-to-face interaction. My father used to drive to every single insured for their renewal meetings. In contrast, even before the pandemic, I had less than fifteen in-person meetings annually—not because I didn't want to meet, but because Millennials like myself were too busy to meet in person.

The Bottom Line

Hopefully, you can now see the importance of consideration and planning for generational differences, preferences, and needs. You need to be crystal clear when addressing and supporting each group. You can no longer have a one-size-fits-all approach to recruiting and retaining employees. By planning your business around employee needs and preferences, you can better compete and attract top talent.

Tailoring your benefits packages, training programs, and workplace culture to each generation's preferences will enhance your agency's appeal as a talent magnet. As I mentioned earlier, getting one great hire will attract more great hires, so adjusting your approach on an individualized basis will pay off in the long run.

CHAPTER 3:
WHY COLLEGE NO LONGER WORKS

The chief value in going to college is that it's the only way to learn it really doesn't matter.

—George Edwin Howes

In November of 2021, the Education Data Initiative reported that "the average cost of attendance for a student living on campus at a public four-year in-state institution is $25,864 per year or $103,456 over four years." However, only 39% of students graduate in four years.

The cost of tuition has increased over 350% since 1963, adjusting for inflation. Why has college become so expensive? Some data suggests that it has to do with colleges turning into profit machines (yes, even public institutions). The same report by Education Data Initiative uncovered that "for-profit schools charge 75% more in tuition when students are eligible for federal loans." Further, "between 1975 and 2005, the number of administrators had increased by 85% and administrative staffers by over 240%." All the while, these institutions are hiring contract professors and shifting a portion of the courses online to save money on staffing. Keep in mind that this was happening before the pandemic.

Meanwhile, housing expenses have increased, and wages have stagnated. In 2019, the median household income was $61,372, while the housing price in 2018 was $400,000. And even if students found a job after graduating from college, it still took them an average of six months to find a full-time job. Companies often hire more part-time workers to avoid paying for benefits.

The news is not good for Millennials or Gen Z and has all sorts of ramifications for their future. It's also not good for our industry. Other industries might be offering higher compensation packages right out of the gate, which have become necessary to address the debt situation.

It's hard for agencies to justify higher compensation plans when a college education doesn't translate to any meaningful impact in the agency world.

A few years ago, companies like Apple, Bank of America, and Google made waves by announcing they would no longer have degree requirements for specific jobs. Curiously, they still seem to be the exception to the rule. Many companies still use the degree requirement to screen candidates—a practice that just doesn't make sense anymore.

Think about it. Years ago, we used the degree requirement to weed out hundreds of applicants for a job posting. We had more than we could handle in the workforce, so the obvious answer was more stringent qualifications. We began requiring degrees for a position that didn't previously need one. This practice, known as degree inflation, has come with some unexpected consequences.

Those entry-level insurance jobs that didn't formally require a degree were filled with college graduates. This resulted in agencies offering higher starting salaries that were not in line with the actual value provided to the agency.

Do you require a degree as part of your job requirements? If so, have you ever asked yourself why? Do you require it just because you always have? Honestly, ask yourself what specific skills translate and whether the increased starting salary is worth it. If we're talking writing, math, marketing, and so on, you can pick up some fantastic skills in an $8 course from companies like Udemy. They also offer corporate plans, which could be a great benefit to your existing staff. If you're unsure, now is the perfect time to reconsider whether a degree is necessary.

In 2018, The Society for Human Resource Management (SHRM) stated that "nine in ten employers reported being ready to accept a candidate without four-year college degrees to fill positions in an increasingly tight labor market." The survey also showed that companies are more willing to hire someone with a recognized certification relevant to their industry than a college degree. Our industry has been the exception to this rule in the commercial lines space. The personal lines agencies were much more willing to overlook the degree requirements.

We have an extraordinary imbalance right now. Our broken educational system isn't keeping up with business needs, and companies—especially insurance agencies—are dealing with a tight labor market. Innovative companies are more willing to overlook degree requirements. And in some industries, it works well. For example, tech companies are now more open to hiring talent from shorter tech-training programs or even offering their own educational path through certifications. Google has even developed its programs with a job offer upon completion.

I want to revisit my previous points. While there are some benefits to having college-educated employees, we need to reevaluate whether the benefits outweigh the burden on up-and-coming talent. Do you know the benefits of hiring a college graduate? Did their degree give them skill training needed for the position, or did they simply get an expensive piece of paper?

College degrees often indicate that someone has received a certain level of education in a particular area (i.e., marketing, business communication, or English). They have also been exposed to different ways of thinking, which can be beneficial in positions where creativity or critical thinking skills are necessary. In addition, employers may prefer to hire college graduates because they often come equipped with qualities such as teamwork skills and leadership experience. However, the tightening labor market and talent war are forcing us to reconsider.

Unfortunately for agencies, college degrees are about as effective at preparing individuals for an insurance career as pre-licensing programs. In short, it doesn't translate. Insurance is more about soft skills, aptitude, and coachability. You need talent with problem-solving skills, the right communication style, the ability to navigate conflict resolution, a talent for prospecting, time management mastery, writing skills, and experience with math (and not calculus). The right practical training program can do the rest.

In college, you don't learn anything that is immediately applicable to your initial job duties, including in many university risk management programs. Rather, you must get licensed and learn how to do the job through hands-on experience. College won't teach how to request loss runs, complete ACORD forms, fill out submissions, or even explain a proposal to an insured. It also won't address how to use your agency management system. I could go on and on!

Further, you must recognize the difference between potential employees who graduated with debt and those who did it without. If the applicant has debt, they will likely be searching for positions with higher initial base salaries. They'll also be looking for a corporate ladder that will provide the necessary compensation increases to help service the debt. Raises will mean less because all additional income will service their significant debt. This means they will also be quicker to jump to another agency out of necessity—and it's tough to blame them. Student debt impacts every aspect of life, from basic disposable income to homeownership.

Unfortunately, many college graduates have been led to believe their degree has more value than it does, especially in our industry. They are ignorant of the fact that their degree doesn't provide much value in terms of actual labor for the first year in insurance. They must first get licensed and then learn practical skills and insurance basics. Even if they pick up these new skills quickly, training requires someone else's time, which offsets their productivity. On top of that, their pace will be slower, and they'll make more mistakes. In short, they will be less efficient than their counterparts for a year. And that's under ideal circumstances where there is no downtime and plenty of opportunities to practice.

Unfortunately, we've been indoctrinated to believe that college graduates are more intelligent and contribute more than those who lack degrees. In fact, the agency I used to work for had two tracks for account managers—one for those with degrees and one without. The pay scale was different even though the job responsibilities were the same. Faulty thinking at its finest!

Historically, the industry has treated account managers like second-class citizens within agencies. This distinct separation creates even more inequality and makes it impossible to build a culture that draws others to your organization. To be honest, if I had to decide between two candidates with a college degree as the only separating factor, I'd take the one without the degree seven times out of ten.

Since my agency policy only brings on new-to-industry hires, I have a different set of requirements. I look for aptitude, emotional intelligence, computer literacy, personality fit, attention to detail, problem-solving mindset, and most importantly, grit. If they haven't built up their resilience, I won't hire them. And make no mistake, resilience is a skill that we can learn. If a candidate has all the above, I can train them into a best-in-class account manager very quickly.

It's also important to note that you can easily test for aptitude, personality, computer literacy, and emotional IQ. Attention to detail, grit, and a problem-solving mindset can be vetted through the interview process. And if you're wondering how little I think of college education, almost none of my current account managers have one.

CHAPTER 4:
WHY PEOPLE DON'T WANT TO GO INTO INSURANCE

Businesses have to make gestures that go beyond words. Persuasion no longer works.

—John Gerzema

If you can't sell Millennials and Gen Z from outside the industry an insurance career, you surely can't sell them on coming to work for your agency. And therein lies the problem: selling. The art of persuasion. I'm going to stand on my soapbox for a moment, so bear with me. It's just a slight detour into the subject of selling and persuasion. Trust me, it will make sense.

Depending on your age and whether you have taken an interest in mastering sales, you have heard of or seen Zig Ziglar in person. He had a following—almost a cult—and was known as the master of teaching top selling techniques. The memorization of sales scripts, getting them to say yes more than they say no. Anyone?

First, let me just say he was undeniably a master, and he still has a devout following. Don't get me wrong. His tactics and techniques worked. That said, please note the past tense: "worked." If you are or know someone who is a boomer or Gen Xer, they may argue that the techniques still work like a charm. And I wouldn't argue. If it works for you, use it. However, I would beg you to reexamine your tactics.

With the age of the internet, consider your generational audience. If you're trying to recruit a Gen Xer, guess what: they don't trust your salesmanship. If you're speaking to Millennials or Gen Zers, they are far savvier about your tactics. Trying to sell someone on anything through memorized scripts and how things were done before the internet is guaranteed to be less successful.

To be brutally honest, the insurance industry has a branding problem, and it's 100% our fault. The statistics show that less than 4% of Millennials and Gen Z would even consider the insurance industry. Out of the four million college graduates, only 160,000 might consider us.

We don't currently have the number of people who aren't college graduates. But since we have ignored them to this point, it's not even worth adding them to the potential pool.

The 160,000 graduates that might consider the insurance industry have over 36,000 agencies and 6,000 insurance companies to pick from. And that doesn't even include the other industries and jobs they get to evaluate. The point is that they have options, and the insurance industry seems to be one of those jobs that people just happen to fall into. You rarely hear someone say they intentionally went into insurance.

This branding problem stems from a variety of issues, including workplace culture, a lack of diversity and growth opportunities, and just the idea that insurance is a boring job.

Now consider the traditional gender-defined roles. Let me paint a picture. Imagine you have just divorced your third wife and are trying to woo a woman. You have unkempt hair. You're overweight, have a history of insisting women can only perform specific roles, and insist that women give more while receiving less. You're going to be a lonely guy for a while.

So, let's connect the dots. Our industry is mainly comprised of women, and their roles have historically been within the account management space with little opportunity to pivot toward sales or even senior management. On top of that, we tend to value producers so much that we're willing to excuse their behaviors and view the supporting talent as expendable. In fact, I have personal knowledge of one agency that allowed a producer to go through eleven account managers over three years. He literally drove talented women away from the organization between his demanding nature, odd hours, and inappropriate sexual overtures. This situation created a branding nightmare for the agency, which continues to this day.

Most women are long past accepting inequality and inexcusable behavior in the workplace. They, too, have other options, and other industries have done a better job addressing the inequality in gender roles. Unfortunately, even if your agency has made progress, the industry at large hasn't communicated advancements and improvements in our culture.

Negative perceptions about upward mobility aren't just limited to female candidates. In general, there's an overwhelming belief that the industry career path is limited. 85% of the agencies in our industry have annual revenues of less than $500,000. When candidates hear about their role, they think of only working for smaller agencies. And even if they interview for the position, they know that they can only go from an assistant account manager to an account manager. Further, there's the notion that if you work for the wrong agency and only learn one industry vertical, you can't pivot elsewhere without going backward.

Other minorities are also significantly underrepresented, especially in senior leadership. If there is no clear vision of a path forward past an existing role, they won't bite. It's wrong to assume that we're past women and minorities having to break ceilings and barriers. If they don't see a potential role model or mentor, they're less likely to be interested in interviewing at your agency. Another issue is that many minorities never make it past the screening stage. We will dive deeper into that in a later chapter.

The last glaring perception by would-be candidates is that insurance is boring. Remember that we have at least one large generation (Millennials) who wants to make a difference. You can't make a difference if you're stuck in processing all day. Many agencies never figure out how to reduce the deskwork so that their people can focus on building relationships and problem-solving. Millennials and Gen Zers are searching for experiences—and exciting, purposeful ones at that. Mindlessly processing from a cubicle doesn't necessarily generate a desirable response.

Now add the messaging from large corporate machines to that. GEICO, State Farm, Farmers—they all have catchy commercials. Those ads stick in our memories and, unfortunately, define a career in insurance with corny taglines or khaki pants and a collared shirt. Not exactly what the next generation of workers has in mind. Small to midsized agencies have also missed the mark with little to no branding and zero outreach efforts. And honestly, it doesn't cost that much to build an online brand presence these days. Millennials and Gen Zers spend a great deal of time on YouTube, Instagram, TikTok, and other streaming or social media platforms—which is where you should be!

The best thing about these platforms is that the advertising and branding cost pennies compared to traditional marketing, and it gets to your targeted audience faster. I will talk more about how to leverage these channels in later chapters, but I want you to know that you can build a more prominent brand presence, no matter your size.

So how should our industry be doing it differently? There's a great book called *The Go-Giver* by Bob Burg. It's a powerful parable about the laws of attracting business. Over the course of a week, the character learns how changing their tactics from "getting" to "giving" results in unexpected returns. The idea is that if you focus on helping people with what they need instead of worrying what it'll get you, you'll benefit in unexpected ways.

As an industry and as individual agencies, we need to change from the Zig Ziglar "getting" mentality. We need to change the "get them to shake their head up and down" or "get them to yes" into giving potential new-to-industry hires a kind gesture, a listening ear, or something they need. And we need to understand that the person you give to may not be the one who returns the gesture but could introduce you to the next person to become your rising star.

The insurance profession of old has changed radically, and we must communicate that. We also must be able to identify precisely what has changed and why. We need to focus on providing value that causes potential employees to dig a little deeper and see the opportunity our industry offers.

CHAPTER 5:
THE OUTSOURCING AND INSURTECH IMPACT

There are downsides to everything; there are unintended consequences to everything.

—**Steve Jobs**

For the past few years, our industry trend has been to outsource and delegate repetitive clerical tasks so that you can focus on what you specialize in or the "money-making activities." As a result, we have gotten rid of seats on the bus. We have removed opportunities from the foundation of our industry and taken away entry-level positions that build knowledge and skill base.

Outsourcing and Insurtech have eliminated entry-level insurance jobs. These jobs were not just menial tasks done by a seat warmer though. They were a means to an end. They were a way for both new hires and management to figure out whether they were a good fit for each other. The unintended consequence of outsourcing these entry-level jobs is the elimination of a training ground in which to further vet talent before investing tremendous resources in them. In short, we could determine if they were going to stay in the business long term and, more importantly, whether we would want them to.

When I started, there were specific entry points into the insurance world. Tasks that would be tedious, boring, and repetitive in nature served as the first rung on the corporate ladder. The ability to listen, follow instructions, work hard, and pay attention to details is what propelled you to the next level. In short, the agency had time to evaluate your skillset at a lower wage before investing a higher compensation and training in you. A clear starting point and career path gave new hires time to acclimate and managers time to evaluate.

Now, two of the five roles (certificate processors and technical assistants) have been eliminated. As a result, agencies are forced to take big risks with compensation and time on unproven candidates for higher-functioning roles. This makes hiring out of college especially precarious. As a rule of thumb, recent graduates are likely to job hop within their first twelve months in the workforce. Green in talent, these students start off thinking, "It's just my first job" as opposed to "This could be my career."

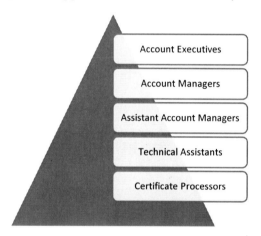

So why did things change? Simply put, in a capitalist society, businesses will always search for a way to do things better, faster, and for more profit. We can't stop progress. Publicly traded agencies, where sustained organic growth was hard to come by, needed to make up ground by improving EBIDTA (Earnings Before Interest, Taxes, Depreciation, and Amortization), especially for their quarterly earnings calls. This drove them to research numerous alternatives, from small business units to ultimately outsourcing the lower entry positions the industry used to rely on to create longer career paths for employees.

There was a lot of heavy lifting early on, but the numbers were penciled out. Outsourcing proved that agencies could ship entry-level jobs overseas, where labor was cheaper and faster, and workers were eager to pick up the work. Then Insurtech was introduced and proved automation could do these tasks even faster.

In the back office, we outsourced non-customer-facing processes. Some of the tasks that impacted entry-level jobs were:

- Certificates processing

- Policy checking

- Loss run requesting

- Proposal creation

- Online submissions

- Endorsement processing

Then Insurtech offered solutions like e-signatures and self-service options on apps and comprehensive agency-management platforms. Customers can now add or delete vehicles or create their own certs, and we provide renewal updates online. Completing supplemental applications went from being a manual labor nightmare to a simple data-bridging exercise. AMS proposal templating has also radically improved. All these changes further reduced the clerical duties of the entry-level role.

Outsourcing and automation can be of great value when appropriately deployed, but most agencies are still fumbling.

Now consider your new hire and employee experience when outsourcing is used. Do you have a specific plan for that new-to-industry hire that allows them to meaningfully contribute in their first six months? Without that early experience from entry-level industry positions, a new hire will have knowledge gaps, no matter how far they go in your agency. Your existing staff may have been capable of training them in specific entry-level tasks, but can they train a carbon copy of themselves that's capable of tackling more complex tasks right out the gate?

With so many employees retiring, we need a deep bench. The problem is that the players on the bench need to be ready to play on day one. Remember, baby boomers are our largest generation aside from Millennials. Baby boomers are now between the ages of fifty-seven and seventy-five years old. We know we need to feed the labor pipeline, yet there's so much to learn, and the stakes are high. With outsourcing, new hires are immediately forced into highly stressful and complex roles with little guidance. Given Gen Z's makeup, this is like walking a tight rope in 20 mph winds over a fiery pit while juggling knives.

Individuals who can handle that kind of pressure and responsibility are few and far between.

Further, that kind of employee is going to want to rise quickly in the ranks. How many agencies even have the capacity for that next step? This top talent is coveted and will be fielding offers from your competitors left and right, and you'll likely lose them without a proper plan.

So, is it possible for you to offer enough incentives, challenges, and upward mobility for this person? The answer is yes, but we'll discuss how later. Further, you need to attract a pipeline of these unicorns so that you can build your systems, people, processes, and profit at scale.

It's essential to recognize that each new solution our industry comes up with has potential benefits and many unintended consequences. However, Insurtech and outsourcing have been around long enough that the consequences are no longer ambiguous. The great news is that this next generation of insurance professionals will consider our industry if we demonstrate how we will adequately equip them for the job.

Building a robust onboarding and training program that mitigates the Insurtech and outsourcing consequences is a lot of work, but it's not optional.

I'd like to use my company as an example. Because my team heavily leverages outsourcing, and given the size of my agency, I have eliminated rungs on the corporate ladder. As a result, I have employees ready to grow into more complex roles. Still, sometimes the position does not exist because it's occupied by another employee. They have gone as far as they can go with me unless the person above them leaves, or we land a tremendous amount of new business in a short timeframe.

The fact that I can onboard and train so quickly (and well) means that I don't have to try to hold that employee hostage. We have an agreement with our team. If it's not a fit for them, I receive a couple of months' notice, giving me time to hire, onboard, and train someone to take over. In return, they receive a glowing recommendation from me (which has been earned; if it hadn't, they would have just walked). I will also reach out to my entire network on their behalf to set up interviews for them at other agencies. If I can get their replacement trained faster, I will pay them the balance owed for the remaining time left, and they can take a vacation before starting the new job.

My credibility is bolstered when employees see that my efforts to reach out to other agencies were extremely successful (I booked seven interviews within an hour) and ultimately got them placed with quality agencies that had their desired roles. That is how I have been able to overcome the shorter corporate ladder. Again, knowing that I am committed to their success and growth in this industry has strengthened our culture as an agency, even with people leaving.

The disappearance of entry-level positions, and even some more advanced tasks, will only accelerate. If you think this is a problem now, just wait for the changes that will come over the next forty-eight months. You shouldn't just develop action plans based on the current Insuretech solutions available; you must anticipate what's coming down the pipe and plan accordingly.

CHAPTER 6:
DIVERSITY AND INCLUSION

We are building products that people with very diverse backgrounds use, and I think we all want our company makeup to reflect the makeup of the people who use our products.

—Sheryl Sandberg

Allow me to start with a disclosure: I do not fall into the politicized definition of "woke." However, I have become aware of an enormous missed opportunity in the insurance industry. Agencies cannot win the talent war without tapping into the qualified and underrepresented minority community. If you're unsure about the statistics and evidence, let's start with the fact that 80% of our industry's employees are white. Now, I touched on diversity in a previous chapter, but now we need to take a hard look at the business opportunities left on the table that a lack of diversity causes.

For argument's sake, even if you don't care about the people (which I hope you would), you most certainly care about the bottom line or EBIDTA (Earnings Before Interest, Taxes, Depreciation, and Amortization). According to Mckinsey, a company's EBITDA increases by 1% for every 10% more racially diverse its senior team becomes. Further, studies show time and again that consumers want to do business with organizations and people they trust—those that match their values and culture. If agencies don't start addressing this, clients will start placing business with those that do.

The insurance industry is a people business. So why haven't we had more diversity? First, consider legacy. Remember when I mentioned that most people working in insurance didn't pick it as a first career choice? We most often fall into the business. In many cases, this is due to decades and decades of agencies being passed down as a family business.

Historical Association

Throughout history, professions have been handed down from one generation to the next. Even our surnames have some professional historical context. John Smith had a great-great-grandfather who was a blacksmith, and James Baker had a great-great-grandfather who was a baker. More recently, you find that a son may follow their dad and grandfather's footsteps and join the military, work as an electrician, or be a pilot. Historically, women would become teachers because their mothers were teachers. We have often followed a path of least resistance, on which we know we will have the support and expertise of our parents to guide us along the way. The insurance industry is no different.

As a result, the insurance industry has a long history of being predominately white/Caucasian-owned and operated. The first generation of insurance professionals was predominantly Caucasian, so the following generations were as well. Diversity and inclusion efforts have been slow. Not because we don't want to be diverse and inclusive—on the contrary. There's simply a lot to catch up on.

There hasn't been a long history of formal education, opportunity, networking, or support in the industry for nonwhite talent compared to those opportunities for white owners and operators. So how do you break free from the pattern of legacy and encourage diversity and inclusion?

It's Who You Know

If your rising talent has never met anyone they like and trust in insurance, how will they learn about the opportunity? Agencies and carriers haven't worked trade fairs and developed meaningful relationships within communities with large minority populations nearly as much as they should have. There's no way diverse candidates will find their way into our industry if we don't meet them where they are. Further, if you're introduced to the industry but can't find anyone of your skin color or gender in leadership positions, you'll likely gravitate toward an industry that you believe will offer that opportunity.

It's a vicious cycle that needs to be broken. You can't attract a diverse talent pool if you aren't diverse. However, to become diverse, you need new, diverse talent to get on board. You have to start somewhere. My agency works in construction, which has a sizable Hispanic population. I have two bilingual employees. They were able to develop deeper relationships with our Spanish-speaking construction clients. Ultimately, their linguistic ability translated into a significant referral business we would have never gotten otherwise.

These employees came to me through typical recruiting methods. However, this is not to say you cannot use nontraditional methods to recruit diverse talent. On the contrary, if you bring some awareness to the process, you have the battle half won.

By awareness, I mean open your agency to getting involved in minority-dominated communities. Get involved with the community colleges and high schools in the area. Ask your team members whether they would like to join and offer to facilitate an after-school activity, social event, or awareness campaign. You need to make sure you're providing the community with value beyond an introduction to the insurance industry. If it's all about your agency, it isn't about them. (Remember the giving mindset?) My agency has given short seminars unrelated to insurance but sponsored by the industry, and it doesn't take much work to get that off the ground. Reaching out to influential leaders in the community will not be difficult, and they will likely welcome a professional services company coming in to help their community.

My personal philosophy is that you need to first be present, show you care, and then educate on the industry's opportunities, which we can validate with success stories.

My employees' ability to connect culturally and bridge the language gap became a unique strength of my agency not found in many of our competitors. Interestingly, culture and language are common barriers we must overcome to build trust. Bringing minorities into the fold will go a long way toward easing the talent crisis. But before you tackle that, I would strongly suggest addressing or confronting our industry's conscious and unconscious biases, as this will provide us with a window into the potential solution. Failure to do so will likely increase the odds against this initiative. But we as agencies have a few stumbling blocks that need to be confronted both by education and by eliminating leaders who purposefully continue to exclude the minority community from opportunities they otherwise deserve.

The bottom line is whether your talent will successfully harness a diverse workforce is dependent on your agency's adoption of a well-thought-out diversity strategy. There is a saying: "What you focus on expands." Suppose we focus less on a "no tolerance antidiscrimination policy" and more on a diversity and inclusion policy with specific objectives, supported by a strong why and action steps to achieve the goal. Not only will the results be noticeably different but the specific behaviors in the agency will also become part of the culture. Those who cannot adapt will self-eliminate.

So, what does a proactive inclusion and diversity process and policy look like for the insurance industry? First, agencies need to start a dialog. Too often, we see companies or agencies state that they have a "diverse" workforce, yet when you start to ask questions, you soon discover a lack of understanding about inclusion and how its absence negatively impacts the community and, more specifically, our talent magnet. Again, we should put an emphasis on this simply because it's the right thing to do, but sometimes leadership needs to be motivated by more than that.

One way to approach this dialog is to think about it in terms of dimensions. There are many different dimensions to diversity, including race, ethnicity, gender, disability, and sexual orientation. Once you have identified these dimensions, you can begin to ask more questions. In the best-case scenario, you have employees that feel comfortable sharing their personal experiences to educate your team.

How do your employees identify? What are their experiences? Do they feel included in the workplace? How might you be able to improve things? Listening is the first step in gathering data and identifying the true needs within your agency. Are women paid less than their male counterparts despite doing the same job? Maybe you have a diverse staff but no minorities in a leadership position. Every agency's challenges will be unique, but to become a magnet for diverse talent, you must demonstrate to your own employees that their voices will be heard, and that equal opportunity truly does exist within the agency. Bear in mind that I am not talking about quotas. I don't believe we should fill roles specifically because of a need to become more diverse. Rather, I think we need to be open to the possibility that we aren't recognizing the talent in front of us because of some unconscious bias. This also means that your agency needs to have objective metrics to compare employees to one another. That alone takes a lot of work.

When you include your employees in the dialog rather than dictate a new policy, you'll surely get more involvement and better direction. Once you have opened a line of communication, act. You shouldn't just start the dialog and then thank everyone for their input. You need to digest the information and leverage your team to identify areas that can facilitate a diverse staff, which will ultimately attract far more new-to-industry hires than the status quo.

A great starting point is to explain to your team the major benefits of a more diverse team. Studies have shown that diverse teams produce faster problem-solving, higher employee engagement, reduced turnover, better recruitment, and increased profitability. According to Glassdoor, 67% of job seekers said a diverse workforce is important when considering job offers. Additionally, companies with significantly diverse management teams have 19% higher revenue than their counterparts, according to Bosting Consulting Group.

Another great way to build diversity in your agency is to use diverse job boards such as Diversity Jobs or Hirepurpose, which is dedicated to veterans and military spouses, along with RecruitDisability, which is a job board for those with disabilities. You should also consider offering targeted internships for members of minority communities and investing in the communities without expecting things in return. At the same time, I strongly recommend having a diverse interview panel. That often means including those individuals not on the leadership team but representative of the workforce you're looking for. Ultimately, you'll need a desired outcome, action steps along the way, a way to measure progress, and absolute buy-in from your team.

As I close this chapter, I want to speak to those agencies who may already be doing a lot of things right and might take offense to the broad-brush approach I have taken. For your employees, feelings aren't fact, but perception is reality. What I mean by this is you may not have a diversity issue in your office, but it doesn't stop some people from feeling that you do. Proactively addressing those concerns and leveraging data to get an accurate assessment of your performance will help build not only an empathetic culture but also a set of guardrails to ensure your agency doesn't start to go off course. Until you do that, the perception within and outside your agency may continue to be that your culture is exclusionary by design. Once you're past that hurdle, you'll find that even more out-of-industry candidates will gravitate toward your agency. The time to act is now—not only with your diversity and inclusion initiatives but also with building your talent magnet as a whole.

CHAPTER 7:
WHY YOU CAN'T PUT THIS OFF

The danger of venturing into uncharted waters is not nearly as dangerous as staying on shore, waiting for your boat to come in.

—Charles F. Glassman

Chapter 7 is short because, well, honestly, if you look around your office, you already know why you can't put this off. Our talent war continues to accelerate at breakneck speeds, with the Great Resignation and older employees aging out of the workforce. But to put it in context, consider the following.

The well-capitalized companies are desperate for talent. They have a war chest that enables them to pay 20% more than smaller agencies and offer additional benefits. How will you compete if it isn't through salary or other benefits? Additionally, the endless retirements each year further exacerbate the problem. We expect there will be approximately four hundred thousand workers retiring over the next few years. Your competitors are already planning, restructuring, and implementing changes. If you haven't begun that process, they have a massive head start. And make no mistake, they are coming for your A-players.

If you aren't prepared, your A-player will be poached, and you'll either overpay for a B-player (if you can find one) or bring in a new-to-industry hire. What will this cost your business? If it happens once, maybe you won't notice because you'll find a way to pick up the slack. However, you'd create the problem where new industry hires are now trained by the B-player and not the A-player. It's like the game of telephone. Where does your retention rate go when your B-player now handles top accounts and trains the new hire with lower quality? Further, what happens to your workplace morale and your customer experience?

Other agencies will inevitably court your existing staff, who will see the writing on the wall if you aren't building a talent magnet. Employees want to be at an agency that is committed to growing their people, purpose, and profit. With those expanding, there would be little reason for an employee to look elsewhere.

Back to the sense of urgency required to be successful. Remember that Millennials and Gen Z will comprise north of 80% of the workforce by 2025. Time is short, the task is significant, and your top competitors already have an eighteen-month head start on your agency. You must put more resources, time, and effort toward your talent magnet than you have ever done before.

I recognize that diverting capital and resources to this challenge can be a scary proposition, but don't worry. I'm not suggesting you throw your entire marketing and advertising budget out the window. On the contrary, you should simply reallocate a portion of your new business revenue to support this effort. Most of what is required doesn't require the financial war chest you think it does. And it's important to know that the cost of inaction will be far greater than any money you risk by investing in your talent magnet.

CHAPTER 8:
WHERE TO BEGIN

There will come a time when you believe everything is
finished. Yet that will be the beginning.

—Louis L'Amour

Before you build a better talent magnet, you must figure out how effective the existing one is. Surprisingly, most agencies don't know what they have going in their favor, let alone what would make them a magnet for top talent. And those that think they know are often wrong. What you think is attractive may be entirely out of step with what top talent currently wants. For example, would you believe that the number one requested benefit by Millennials is pawternity? Not paternity, pawternity—as in you just got a new puppy and want to take time off work to help her acclimate. I'm not kidding. This is number one, above flexible work schedules, student loan repayment, and even free beer. I'd like to think I'm pretty in tune with the needs of Millennials but that one threw me for a loop.

So, before you list out what you think are your attractive features and benefits, consider doing something with a little more analysis. Take an anonymous survey of your current team. Ask them about management, opportunities for growth, technology, challenges, flexibility, and so on. Whether you bring in an outside consultant or simply use an online survey program, just let your team know the intent and get the necessary feedback about the state of your agency. Find out what specifically makes this a great place to work or a place that they are thinking about leaving. Is there enough vacation time? Do they enjoy the management style? Do they wish there was more accountability? Do they like the snacks in the break room? Do they want a better retirement plan or a more flexible benefits structure? Do they feel they are being paid enough? All this feedback will factor into your action plan to build a talent magnet.

Next, find information about your exes. No, not that kind of ex.

Reach out to former employees that left on a voluntary basis and find out why they really departed. If you had managed to complete exit interviews, go back and review them. I also suggest interviewing existing staff for their thoughts on why the team member left. You might need to do this anonymously or be very transparent that what they say will be used to help improve management and won't be held against them. And be prepared to hear answers that call into question both your leadership and overall offering. Enjoy your humble pie. My brother and I once brought in an independent consultant that sent us home with about a dozen humble pies each. After the massive stomachache they gave us, we made the necessary changes to shore up our culture and better empower our team.

Again, you need to discover the strengths and weaknesses of your talent magnet based on what *they* think, not what you think. You also need to understand your opportunities and threats. Do you have a hidden strength you can leverage for more opportunities to attract top talent? Or do you have a weakness that will threaten your future goals, cause employees to leave dissatisfied, and negatively impact the agency's brand? One thing I always took for granted was my sense of duty to my team. It's just how I'm wired. My team members don't doubt that I would go to war for them, personally or professionally—and they've seen me do it! After recognizing the importance of this, we decided to make it a defined benefit of coming to Goodman Insurance. Now, whenever we interview candidates, our team members will bring this up proactively. Candidates walk away knowing two things for sure: employees at my agency are valued for who they are, not what they do, and I will never let a client, prospect, producer, or business partner disrespect them. Given that so many service team members have felt like second-class citizens compared to their producer counterparts, this simple act of decency and respect is a needle-mover.

Once you have as much information as you can gather, put together your State of the Union (State of Your Talent Magnet) and present your findings to the team. See if the findings, both past and present, are reflective of your current offering. If not, clarify further and adjust accordingly. At this point, you'll still have more questions than answers, but you'll start to understand what made team members leave and what's keeping current team members around. If you're anything like me, ideas will start to flood in that you'll want to immediately implement. *Stop.* Digest the information and let it sit. Hold your initial ideas loosely, as they may not line up with what your current or future team members want. There are a lot more things to consider before starting construction on your new talent magnet.

CHAPTER 9:
YOUR EXISTING CULTURE

Growing a culture requires a good storyteller. Changing a culture requires a persuasive editor.

—**Ryan Lilly**

Before you can attract the right talent to match your culture, you need to fully understand what your culture is.

We all have an organizational culture, whether we're aware of it or not. It's a semiconscious set of assumptions about how the world works that is reinforced throughout our lives by our experiences in different organizations. These may be cultural artifacts, behaviors, or beliefs that we see around us every day. Organizational cultures often tend to go unquestioned because they exist at such a subconscious level for most people.

Culture represents the collective behavior of the individuals within an organization, including their language and words, actions and nonactions, values, and norms. Culture can be seen as the underlying pattern of behavior that guides, shapes, and directs what an organization does.

Not all organizations have a strong culture. In fact, many organizations don't know what their culture is. Or if they do, they lack the ability to accurately define it in words that others can understand. Many newer companies may also find themselves without a well-defined organizational culture until a significant amount of time has passed and a clear organizational identity takes hold.

Assessing Your Current Culture

As an agency owner, it's crucial to assess your culture and ensure you understand the dynamics. You need to identify your cultural strengths and weaknesses. For example, does your team operate like a rigid agency from the 1960s, or do you have a more modern, collaborative operational style? Do you have cliques? Do you sponsor routine activities like lunches, parties, picnics, or holiday gift exchanges? Then, are these strengths or weaknesses? What about the sales-driven culture? Are account managers and producers assigned new business goals, or are account managers simply focused on taking care of existing client needs? How do you know what kind of culture you have?

Once again, we turn to surveys for the answer. Anonymous surveys, of course. You can create a survey specific to your organization with custom questions or use a free template from SurveyMonkey.com. In your survey, ask your direct reports to complete the following questions:

- In which of these ways do you find that [organization] is different from other places you have worked?

- What are the new things you have learned since working for [organization]?

- If you had to describe [organization] in three words, what would they be?

- How does [organization] compare to other companies you have worked for in terms of being a fun place to work? A boring place to work? An ethical place to work? A stressful place to work?

The best way to get started with this process is simply asking them and listening. Listen without bias and without making immediate assumptions. The survey is meant to get an unfiltered and honest response to both strengths and weaknesses and inspire changes that could put the agency in a better position for the next generation of insurance professionals. Eat that humble pie! Don't argue with the answers or try to explain them away, simply digest the information. Then, take the information and own it.

Culture

We have already asked some important questions about your business, but I have a few more that relate specifically to your company culture. For each question that you're not sure about or you answer in a negative way, make a plan to address the issue and take action:

- Do your team members have friendships with other employees that extend outside of work? You know you have a strong culture if employees want to hang out together after work hours.

- Do you have problem team members that take away from the culture? Ignoring high-drama employees because they are high producers can kill your culture.

- Could everyone in the office define the culture? Ask your employees what your cultural strengths and weaknesses are.

- Do you have open discussions about challenges and strategies that include all employees? You can't have honest conversations with producers and not include account managers.

- Is mentorship taking place? We can all learn something from those around us. One person might be great with customer retention while another may be a community organizer. Be sure to fit new talent with someone they can connect with and learn from.

- Is healthy debate commonplace? This is different from conflict and necessary for exploring and discovering the best ideas and strategies for moving forward possible.

- Do you have the full participation of team members during meetings? A checked-out employee can affect the morale of the rest of the team. If they were previously engaged during team meetings and then suddenly lost interest, there may be something going on with them that you need to address.

- Do employees feel trusted to execute their duties without micromanagement?

- What benefits are you providing? If you have a group of pet lovers, are they allowed to bring their pet to the office? Some other widespread benefits that don't cost a dime are "dress-down" days, long lunches, and an early close on Fridays.

- Is giving back to the community something that is executed agency-wide? Team community involvement is great for bonding and visibility. Survey some important causes to support, then commit to getting involved as a team.

- Do employees feel like they can attend important events for their children and other family members? This can be tricky at certain times of the year. Still, if you can make a concerted effort to support team members so they can participate, they will appreciate you. Consider a rotating calendar or timeshare. Encouraging employees to donate hours or days will result in a more collaborative and supportive environment in general.

Remember: either you define your culture, or your culture will define you. If your culture has already defined you, and you don't like what you discovered, it's time to make some changes.

Creating New Culture or Redefining the Existing Culture

There are several things to consider if you are a new agency or if the input from the team necessitates the reshaping of your current organizational culture. First, revisit your core values and how you incorporate them into daily activities. Second, think about what makes you unique or different from local competitors. Third, reflect on whether your management style supports the culture you have or the culture you want. Finally, assess if critical influencers in the company model the culture or behaviors that support your belief structure. If not, are they willing to grow and change?

The process may seem like a lot to unpack, but you can break it down and eat the elephant one bite at a time.

Your Management Style

Anne Mulcahy, the CEO of Xerox, once said, "Employees who believe that management is concerned about them as a whole person—not just an employee—are more productive, more satisfied, more fulfilled. Satisfied employees mean satisfied customers, which leads to profitability."

Because managers are responsible for leading their teams following organizational goals, they must model behaviors aligned with agency values. Do managers act as role models? Do they represent the core values when working with others or acting alone? What kind of coaching opportunities do employees receive to help them grow within the organization? Is there room for improvement in how management acts out each value so that every team member knows where they stand and what steps are needed for growth?

Some of the more relevant aspects of management and culture to consider include how mistakes and confrontation are handled and whether employees can speak candidly. In times of stress or urgency, mistakes can happen. Life happens, and unexpected events could put a project behind schedule even when your teams deliver excellent results normally.

So how do you handle those inevitable human errors? We don't want to implement punitive actions for minor slip-ups, but managers and leaders must keep time horizons in mind when developing a plan of improvement for any team member who made a mistake. It often makes sense to take corrective action without issuing formal disciplinary actions. Formal disciplinary action and performance improvement plans tend to be the way we prepare an employee for a nonvoluntary exit from the company, and they know it. Instead, take proactive steps to coach your team, keeping in mind their personal circumstances or the challenges presented to their generation. I actually prefer individual monthly meetings with team members over formal reviews, although those do serve their purpose as well. Addressing these issues head-on will obviously have the potential to create conflict. There are also other aspects of life—i.e., relationship troubles, mental health, or financial struggles—creating negative conflict that further exacerbates the issue.

Unfortunately, negative conflict (as opposed to productive conflict) is another issue that seems to be on the rise. Frustrated customers or employees embattled over politics, for example, can create confrontation. You should have a clear policy on handling confrontation when it comes up. Do you actively address issues beforehand, or do you become a referee once words fly? Do you get involved at all or let them work it out? If the confrontation is with a customer, that's probably different from an intraoffice disagreement. The point is that your culture and values should be consistent when working through your management style.

Lastly, do your employees feel safe enough to speak candidly? This can range anywhere from a disagreement on a process all the way up to being hurt by a comment or decision management has made. If they don't feel safe sharing with you, they will likely be talking to someone else in the agency. You don't want yes men/women, you want confident individuals that care more about improving the agency than protecting your ego.

Address Your Weaknesses before Recruiting

If you currently have a culture (or reputation) where inappropriate behavior by producers is tolerated or maybe favoritism and nepotism are rampant, you'll need to get that rectified before accelerating your recruitment efforts. I know of an agency that made some drastic changes and then had employees write reviews six months later, highlighting those changes and how they had improved the work environment.

To attract top talent, you must demonstrate what kind of culture you want to build from day one. Make sure everyone has a voice in this discussion so that you get the input of the people it affects the most. I would place even more importance on millennial and Gen Z input, as they will represent the majority of your agency in a couple of years.

The Benefits Your Employees Actually Want

The current trend when attracting talent is to incorporate the hot button of "flexibility" in our brand. Due to the pandemic, agencies are offering flexible work options for office or remote preferences. They also offer flexible schedules so employees can work four ten-hour days or five eight-hour days. However, when you consider flexibility and your culture, you should really look at what you're trying to accomplish and whether what you currently offer meets the needs of the talent marketplace.

A word of caution: If your culture embraces flexibility, and you offer the same options as your competition, good for you. You aren't behind the curve, but you still don't stand out.

It's also important to consider what flexibility means to employees, not just what it means to you. When employees and candidates say they want flexibility, they often mean they want to be trusted. They want the ability to meet goals and exceed expectations on their terms, not necessarily change how many hours they work per week. They want flexibility in communication, not to be forced into video meetings if an email, call, or—better yet—Slack message is sufficient.

Employees are tying flexibility to well-being. So perhaps your culture should embrace the latter. LinkedIn has transformed its culture to include well-being as a top priority. They offer mental health services, company-wide end-of-year breaks, and meeting-free days. These flexible changes have been well received and set the company up as one of the best places to work.

No matter what you choose to do, make sure your culture and the intangible benefits it offers line up with the marketplace requirements. More importantly, you must deliver on what you promise for both potential candidates and your existing staff. But to do that, you must also develop an organizational growth mindset that's equipped to deal with the continuous change organizations are facing today. No matter where your culture is, it needs to be prepared to evolve as technology, values, and generational objectives change.

CHAPTER 10:
DEVELOP AN ORGANIZATIONAL GROWTH MINDSET

Change is the only constant in life.

—**Heraclitus**

The pace of change in our industry has increased exponentially. Practices from ten years ago are no longer relevant, and those from twenty years ago are archaic. So, if you say you have a growth mindset, but you do not embrace change, you need to reconsider your perspective. A growth mindset embraces change and always strives to improve.

A growth mindset isn't strictly limited to profits, sales, or the number of accounts. Carol Dweck, a Stanford University professor and author, defines it in two ways:

- **A growth mindset.** "The belief that an individual's most basic abilities and skills can be developed through dedication and hard work—brains and talent are just the starting point."

- **A fixed mindset.** "The belief that an individual's basic abilities and skills, their intelligence and their talents, are just fixed traits."

A growth mindset is more about embracing and learning from challenges, realizing that we are not made of stone but clay—moldable and capable of change. It builds resilience and allows you to bounce back and accept criticism while aiming to hit better benchmarks for performance. Further, when you have a growth mindset organization, where "that's just the way we've always done it" isn't the first answer to every question, employees are more likely to report favorable company views.

Dweck's research found that employees in growth mindset organizations are:

- 47% more likely to see their colleagues as trustworthy

- 34% more likely to feel a strong sense of ownership and commitment to their companies

- 65% more likely to say their companies support risk-taking

- 49% more likely to say their companies foster innovation

She also reported that these employee engagement indicators "correlate with higher financial returns." So, while a growth mindset isn't focused on sales and profits, it can lead to them.

Become an expert on this concept, model it, and then require it from your team. Don't worry about impostor syndrome or failing in front of your staff. You, as the leader, must be vulnerable, accept feedback, and provide them a safe environment to build this new way of living.

A growth mindset requires experiential learning, not theoretical exercises. When you consider your talent magnet, think about seeking out natural learners, as they will be much more likely to embrace these changes (even if they are far away from the target mindset). This takes us back to why a degree isn't necessary. A degree requirement comes from a fixed mindset. However, if you seek out people's "capacity and not pedigree," you will be way ahead of the game. When you find people with a commitment to learning, who will build their skill set and rub off on others, they will help your agency accelerate the growth mindset required to adapt to and overcome future market challenges.

Your culture must allow for risk-taking and failure as you provide employees the opportunity to develop skills outside of their typical work set. For an industry focused on mitigating risk, this can seem like a scary proposition. However, we all learn from our mistakes, and it starts at the top.

For example, my employees know some of my biggest failures, insecurities, and areas for improvement. They see me putting in the work and know I can be equal parts humble, vulnerable, and optimistic—with just a touch of grit. My team is more motivated to make changes in themselves because they see it first in me, and the same will be true for you. I am so transparent with my improvement areas that I have openly invited my team to stop me midsentence if my communication is falling short. I simply reset and try again.

To illustrate, let me outline how it played out in my agency. Historically, I've had a negative association with conflict. As a coping mechanism, I used to cut myself off from emotion during difficult conversations, especially when addressing performance issues. This coldness would make the person on the receiving end feel like they were in big trouble when really it was just my own insecurity that led to my robot-like delivery. When this happens now, I simply take a moment, communicate what I am feeling, then dive back into the difficult issue at hand. I urge you to test this method out for a month to see the impact. Once you do, I'm sure your staff will start doing the same.

By nurturing learners, fostering strategic risk-taking, and allowing for failures, agencies create a more agile organization that will stay relevant when things change quickly. There will undoubtedly be yet another black swan event like the pandemic, in which business processes needed to shift abruptly into the future. That's why I love the popular mantra, "We win, or we learn." In the end, the growth mindset of your agency will serve as a powerful magnet in today's challenging environment. It becomes quite the story for team members to share when they are talking to family, friends, and other candidates about their experience at your agency. It's vital to equip your team with this mindset when the vision for your agency's future appears less than certain. It will ground everyone with the confidence that they can roll with the punches, no matter what the future holds.

CHAPTER 11:
IDENTIFYING FUTURE AGENCY NEEDS

Never bring a knife to a gun fight.

—The Untouchables

To enable your insurance agency's success and longevity in the talent war, you must clearly understand where you are, where you're going, and what you'll need to get there. And building a talent magnet isn't just about having your house in order. You need to identify roadblocks and threats that could appear down the road and the weapons you'll need to overcome them.

Let's first think about your long-term growth trajectory. A growth trajectory is the course you expect your agency to take over the next few years. Agencies need to look at this as a particular target with metrics. What are you trying to accomplish? What are your future revenue and profitability goals? How many employees will be required, and what kind of space do they need? These are not always easy questions to answer. They require time, effort, and data. In this chapter, we are going to dive into a few potential future needs that could influence your long-term growth trajectory.

Target and Metrics

One area in which many agencies stumble is setting arbitrary goals. Or worse yet, they haven't even figured out what their goals are. How will your agency know what you need if you don't know where you are going? Some decisions will directly impact profitability, while others are more indirect. The key is to give equal attention to both and plan your talent needs and required resources accordingly.

Let's talk about revenue targets for a minute. If it's an aggressive target, do you have team members from both the sales and service sides committing to the plan? If you have aging producers near retirement, they might not be motivated to go all in, which results in them acting more as de facto account managers. Regardless, it's essential to have a plan for bringing in younger producers that can propel the agency forward if you want to meet your target.

However, those younger producers will need to be mentored. Who in your agency will do it? Even if your existing producers are willing to train and mentor these new hires, you likely still need a new sales manager (even if that's you). That sales manager will need to have had a lot of success in bringing in new revenue. But if they're great at what they do, what's the carrot that motivates them to come over? If they are part of your organization already, what impact would moving them from sales activities to managerial responsibilities have on your revenue target? Oh, and don't forget: If your producers are going to bring on new business, it will need to be serviced. Your talent magnet needs to be strong in all areas and departments if you want to increase revenue.

Another option to achieve your growth target is to acquire or merge with other agencies and leverage pooled resources to make more substantial purchases. Mergers and acquisitions can be costly in many ways, so once again, consider the direct and indirect impacts. For example, if you merge with another agency or company, what is their culture? What are the policies and procedures? Maybe it makes sense, but perhaps it doesn't. Will another management layer be required? Will roles need to be eliminated or repurposed? A talent shuffle is inevitable, no matter the direction of the acquisition. How much talent are you prepared to lose post-acquisition because of friction?

Future Agency Niches

We all know what successful niche-focused agencies look like, but what happens if your survival depends on multiple niches? For example, my construction insurance agency was clobbered by the recession in 2008. A prudent play would have been to develop another niche to balance out the books, in case construction collapsed again. Given that the biggest impact was on the residential side of our business, we opted to go a different route and pivot toward more commercial contractors to protect against our downside. But many agencies are starting to realize that pivoting is not enough.

If you know that this is the case, your agency must prepare in advance. Consider the tools you'll need to make this happen. Do you need staff members that are willing to take on the challenge of writing accounts in a new niche while the business model is built? How will you train them? Do you need to modify your process or systems to service a different niche? (The answer is yes.) How will you identify and attract the type of talent who can get in on the ground floor of your new niche? Don't forget to consider the nature of client interaction. Is the way you communicate going to change?

Client Interactions Are Evolving

The pandemic changed how we interact as a society and as an industry—with clients and each other. We went from meeting people for coffee and in-person office meetings to Zoom calls and text messages. Now, granted, we saw a significant shift in communication long before COVID-19. Still, the pandemic accelerated the necessity of changing our methods of interaction.

Before the pandemic, we didn't hesitate to schedule office meetings when needed, even when it felt inconvenient or wasn't top on the list of things to do. Quick email updates and newsletters were good, and texts were better if we needed a response quickly.

Jump to the present, and now people are hungry for direct contact. Those in my generation tend to be sick of Zoom and emails. We want to see faces and have human interactions. However, others found they prefer the remote-work environment and the flexibility that comes with it, especially among parents and younger generations who are looking to relocate to areas with a lower cost of living. Of course, many regions of the world are still working through pandemic-related issues, so it's difficult to predict the future. The point is that you need to consider how you interact and communicate as an organization. Think hard about whether you'll change based on the niche you're in and heading toward, the type of talent you want to attract and keep, and what your organization needs to achieve future goals.

Some niches want face time and entertaining conversation, while others are so busy that they just want you to email or text them with updates. Will you hire a great written communicator who prefers to send emails, a friendly extrovert that thrives on in-person interactions, or a hybrid to take care of your niche's clients? Now that so many service team members want to work remotely, how will you navigate a niche that may require face time for successful client interactions?

Going forward, who will be traveling for in-person meetings? Or has your client base permanently shifted to a more digitally focused presence? The budget and talent needs look different depending on your strategy and goals. Consider:

- Are your interactions going to change from in-person to video?

- Are the number of phone conversations going to increase or decrease?

- Are the number of email conversations going to increase or decrease?

- Who in the organization will be responsible for each type of client interaction?

Communication methods are an area worth giving significant thought to. A lack of quality communication can and will cost your business if you treat it as an afterthought. It's better to plan ahead and adjust later rather than play catch-up after the fact.

Think about who will set the tone for future niche communications. Do you have a consistent master communicator that can effectively teach others to do the same? Do you need someone to map out a specific communication blueprint? Is that an existing team member, a gun for hire, or somebody you'll bring into the organization?

With so much communication taking place via email, phone, text, and more Zoom meetings, is your existing staff upskilled enough to tackle each of these—especially if specific shifts in communication accelerate? For example, Frank loves to communicate with the insured in person. Still, his client base is older, and after the pandemic, they are now more comfortable with video conferencing. Is Frank prepared to permanently shift to video and learn new ways to build rapport through a screen? Does he even want to pursue new clients in this manner? What happens if these clients not only want to interact with the producer through video but with the service team members that operate out of cubicles as well? The equipment is rather inexpensive, but how will you handle the noise issue? Are your team members comfortable being on camera? Maybe that will require a different dress code to present a certain level of professionalism. Maybe they are self-conscious about their appearance.

As you can see, there are many unintended but foreseeable consequences to even a single decision. With that, you also need to look around the corner for other friction points that will need to be addressed.

Friction Points

Part of your agency's success hinges on reducing current friction points, but it also depends on proactively planning for future ones. Of course, we can't foresee everything that might spring up along the way. However, there are some pretty good predictors out there for our industry.

We previously touched on generational preferences with technology, skill sets, work schedules, and advancement. Here is where you can address some pain points in your current practice and ways to improve for your future growth strategy.

For example, my company learned that we weren't ready to shift to remote work during the pandemic. We didn't have the necessary systems in place, like having a business account for Microsoft Teams or Zoom. Perhaps your team's basic computer literacy was lacking, and they struggled to work remotely. Maybe you didn't have an IT person or resource that could help. Maybe you needed to provide additional compensation so remote staff could have faster internet speeds to better accommodate video. With so many workers wanting flexible schedules, it's safe to say we need to plan for optimal remote work. For example, if you hire remote workers, will they be in your time zone or staggered based on the needs of the agency and the preferences of the individual? What standards do you put in for remote work (i.e., dress code, dogs in the room while on a Zoom call, etc.)?

Another potential point of friction is whether your growth strategy includes adding additional producers and account managers. (Again, the answer is yes.) Will this growth create the need for additional layers of management? Consider your current workload. If you are the only one managing every aspect of the business, how effective will you be if you double or triple the work? Will you provide extra compensation for someone on your team to continue with their current workload and also take on a leadership role? If so, will you provide them with further training in this area? How much and at what cost? Will there be turnover because a certain team member feels slighted by not getting that opportunity? In that case, is it better to hire outside the agency?

This brings up the point of whether you'll need more specific players or multifaceted team members. If you plan to recruit new talent, what are the top skills they need to bring to the table? Do you have the runway to train new-to-industry hires, or do you need veterans to jump into complex accounts now? The answer is that you need both. Unfortunately, the budget required for the veteran has increased by 30% since this time last year. If that's out of your agency's budget, do you have a training and development plan to upskill the new hire so they can contribute to your agency immediately?

Do You Need Cross-Functional Team Members?

Given our rapidly changing insurance environment, along with the next generation's desire to find different employment opportunities, you might need to consider cross-functional teams. It can be a great idea for many reasons. It helps make employees more flexible and adaptable, which is key to today's rapid business environment. After all, it's challenging to train replacements for lost staff members when they've only been doing one job the entire time they've worked for your company. Thus, cross-training can lead to cost savings through increased efficiency, better use of resources, and retention of key personnel who otherwise might leave in search of greater opportunities. Another benefit is that if an employee has fulfilled multiple roles before, they may have developed skills in areas where there are shortcomings in the organization or team. And finally, cross-training is generally seen as an opportunity to provide advancement within an organization. The future candidates you want to attract will view this as a benefit, not a burden.

Cross-training is not limited to learning different job functions within a department. It also includes learning the processes, procedures, and coverage issues of other niches in your office.

There are some potential downsides, the largest of which is that it can lead to overwork if not implemented properly. To properly cross-train, you might need an additional team member who can help take on the existing workload. This would provide sufficient time during work hours to ensure cross-training doesn't completely exhaust the learner.

When considering your company's options for cross-training employees, take into account all other factors in addition to the potential benefits and downsides. For example, suppose you have many new recruits who are still being trained but show great potential as future team players. In that case, you might consider waiting until they've been thoroughly introduced to the organization before investing time and resources in cross-training them. Your approach will depend on several variables, including the size of your organization, the nature of your workforce, and the amount of turnover you see over a given time period.

In general, a cross-training approach can be a boon for the company, as well as for employees who are eager to show off their abilities and talents. A-players want A-player opportunities. So, if you currently only have a single rung instead of a full corporate ladder, cross-training and the additional competencies that come with it will be a step in the right direction in the eyes of growth-minded new hires. But you'll need everyone involved to buy into the idea if you want to succeed, which again circles back to your talent magnet. When word gets out that you specifically cross-train team members and thereby make them more valuable in the hiring marketplace, you'll attract more A-players, which is exactly what you want.

CHAPTER 12:
WHAT'S YOUR VALUE PROPOSITION

Make sure everybody in the company has great opportunities, has a meaningful impact, and is contributing to the good of society.

—Larry Page, CEO of Google

When building a talent magnet, you can define your value proposition in many ways. Therefore, it's essential to analyze your value proposition's purpose and nail the messaging, or else you'll end up attracting the wrong kind of people to your agency. There are three focus areas that encompass your value proposition: leadership, compensation packages, and cultural values.

Leadership

We often think solid and decisive leadership is a strong magnet for talent. However, there is more to it than that. Employees of this generation are looking for leaders who also place a high value on collaboration, involving the entire team in both procedure-building, implementation, and decision-making. They also yearn for a leader who is authentic, vulnerable, and humble. Checking all those boxes is a tall order, but if that describes you, it will go a long way toward making up for any of the agency's other shortcomings. Here are some questions you need to ask yourself:

- Does leadership behave appropriately in the office and require it of others? There is a fine line between being part of the team and getting too comfortable with team members. Favoritism and even discrimination or harassment could be overlooked if leadership is too relaxed.

- Does leadership value families and honor the obligations that come with them? Do you say you honor employees who need to stay home with a sick child but then expect the employee to work from home while tending to them?

- Does leadership show vulnerability? Leaders should be able to admit to mistakes and be transparent about corrections.

- Is leadership informed and educated about the issues that matter most to the team? A great example is how organizations helped (or didn't help) when parents were expected to work from home while homeschooling their children during pandemic lockdowns.

- Does leadership offer an environment that can encourage fun and humor? Can you count the daily number of laughs in your office on one hand?

- Does leadership provide a vision that creates adventure, excitement, and meaningful purpose? Stretch goals, purposeful team building, sharing in the wins, and community outreach are great methods for creating the right recipe for success.

- Does leadership actually fix things when they aren't going well? Do they listen and seek to fully understand the situation while valuing team members' insights before acting to solve the problem?

- Does leadership value an office that is comfortable, welcoming, and appealing to its employees? A literal open-door policy can go a long way. A closed office door is a small habit that says, "I am not available to you."

You may offer the highest compensation package among your competitors, but you will not attract top talent if your leadership skills are lacking. In fact, in a recent survey of two thousand people, 63% said they planned to quit in the next twelve months due to poor management.

It's time to throw myself under the bus. Running two growing companies can be challenging, if not downright exhausting. Fortunately, the teams at both of my companies excel at their jobs. But there is a constant push-pull relationship when balancing my time. Not too long ago, my agency team saw less engagement from me due to my focus on a Total CSR product launch. I didn't effectively communicate the importance of that project. Nor did I explain that the reason I felt comfortable shifting my focus was due to their ability to tackle challenges on their own. In short, they were leading themselves. It didn't help that I was a bit scarce on compliments for their wins and connecting those results to the success of our agency. Fortunately, I had a team member who brought this to my attention. I was able to change course and even moved my office right next to theirs to make sure I was more engaged. It involved giving up a window, but I never looked outside anyway. And to be fair, who am I to complain when they're all stuck in cubicles? That simple adjustment brought my leadership back on track and improved the job satisfaction of my team members. It wouldn't have been possible without a key employee feeling comfortable enough to speak the truth. This dovetails perfectly into agency culture.

Determining Your Cultural Values

A great way to begin this process of cultural evaluation is by brainstorming all the values that represent your agency's past successes and future goals. Create a list of at least thirty items at first. Here are some common organizational values to get you started: integrity, service, teamwork, creativity, commitment, trustworthiness, and professionalism. Once you have a list of values, it's time to prioritize them, which will get you going on creating your new culture or defining your existing one.

Initiating Your Values

The next step is to brainstorm what activities and practices could promote each value within the organization. You can even add these items to the agency handbook to keep everyone on task, promoting company-wide success through personal performance. Some categories of how you could live out your agency's core values include:

- **Integrity.** It's essential that we tell our clients they can rely on us and always ensure client confidentiality.

- **Teamwork.** We work best when we collaborate to deliver to our clients promptly.

- **Creativity.** We are known for structuring unique outside-the-box insurance programs that provide our customers with more flexible financing and premium options.

Now that you have identified values, possible activities, and practices to promote within the organization, assess how your values represent current business practices. Are there areas where some employees could use additional support? Is there a gap between what you want to be known for and what values are being demonstrated by your team's current actions?

My agency values deep relationships with our clients' employees and their families. At the same time, our culture is lighthearted, with lots of witty banter and with a few practical jokes mixed in. And our relationships with our clients are better for it. As a result, we try to figure out whether candidates mix in with our culture. We'll ask them about the funniest thing that happened at their job or the craziest client story. We can tell by their demeanor whether they can joke and take a joke. If you mix that person into the group, and they don't mesh well, it will kill the culture for others. We are completely up front about this in our hiring process. We also value change and improvement. Our team members know that I am always looking to adjust and am willing to completely alter the course if something isn't working. We also value that the best idea wins, and it doesn't matter who it came from. I still have veto power but use it sparingly because I trust my team.

Your Unique Proposition

With a defined set of core values and an understanding of how to activate them, you can now focus on communicating what makes your culture unique. How are your people different from those at other agencies?

At our agency, we have ten specific components of our workplace culture that we make sure to communicate to our clients:

- **Our yes means yes.** Our customers know that we keep our commitments, always.

- **Be truthful, helpful, and coachable.** We will always tell them the truth, even when it's uncomfortable.

- **Think relationship before agenda.** We care more about the personal relationship than the professional one.

- **Go beyond what is expected.** In short, we anticipate the need and then aim two steps past it.

- **Communicate with specificity and grace.** We will always be on the side of over clarification and understanding.

- **Lead by example, measure by results.** We look for ways to lead and then measure the specific impact.

- **Deposit more than you withdraw.** We are a team of givers, not takers.

- **Maintain an attitude that inspires.** Our team is resilient and encouraging. You either come in that way, or we help you develop it.

- **Bandwidth is transferable.** We proactively jump in to help team members get projects across the finish line.

- **Mistakes are learning.** We aren't perfect, and we use failures as teachable moments for the entire agency.

You can have ten components like us or simply narrow your list down to three or four aspects that make you stand out. We started with a few and gradually built our list over time as each component became more easily defined. But culture isn't enough. This is the strongest employee market in the history of our business, and if the perception is that your compensation package is not equal to or better than the competition, you'll become extremely vulnerable to poaching, even if the grass being greener is just a mirage.

Employee Compensation

Does your agency value paying employees what they are worth even though you might not be able to compete with the highest-paying agency? In fact, I guarantee you can't. However, you must still monetarily show employees they are valued and provide a competitive compensation package if you want the talent you're looking for to even consider you.

There isn't necessarily a "right" answer when it comes to compensation packages, but it's critical that you're able to explain to prospective hires everything that is included in a compensation package. One of the challenges agencies run into is when they present the job offer and only showcase pay, vacation days, and a rough summary of the employee benefits. I'll tell you right now that every single employee of mine places a value on our Google-esque food and beverage choices. To this day, I haven't found any other agency that specifically asks team members what their favorite snacks and drinks are and customizes accordingly. It's definitely worth mentioning.

When it comes to top performers, agencies tend to underestimate their employees' worth and are somehow surprised when the employee receives a more lucrative offer. The reactive "wait, come back" raise usually doesn't sit well. Further, even if they accept the raise and stay for a while, the sour taste lingers, and that person eventually leaves anyway. With that in mind, you should absolutely make a point of reaching out to recruiters twice a year to make sure your compensation package is in line with your competitors'.

Now, let's circle back to generational differences. Each generation has a different set of values, and the most recent generations value choice in every aspect of their life. One way to be competitive in this aspect would be to offer a menu of benefits. If you allow employees to select benefits that are important to them, you show that you see them as an individual and not just human capital. Your flexibility and willingness to offer customized benefits will set you apart and become a selling point for working in your agency. To simplify it with a silly example, imagine offering a Smoked Meats of the Month Club membership to a vegan. They would obviously rather just take the cash or select something else.

Another great way to show you value employees is to show them a vision of their longevity. Millennials and Gen Zers want training and upward movement. Give them a well-thought-out visual roadmap with training opportunities—don't just say that you offer advancement. Your agency needs to demonstrate the roadmap and allocate a budget for education and training. The education and training need to be meaningful and include insurance skills, soft skills, and even things like financial planning. Offer technology training for senior staff. Be transparent in your budget allocation and your intentions. If you're spending less than 2% of your revenue on employee development, you're in for a rude awakening. Your value proposition must include investing both time and money in your team members.

Hopefully, by now you can see how all three areas (leadership, culture, and compensation) must be in balance to present a clearly defined and attractive value proposition that will be easy to convey to new talent. If your team isn't enjoying the benefits of your professed value proposition, it won't pass the smell test with candidates.

CHAPTER 13:
YOU BETTER WALK THE WALK

You need to be ready to lead by example and
live up to those values in every way.
Every. Single. Day.

—Sabrina Horn

The *Oxford English Dictionary* writes that a hypocrite is "a person who pretends to have virtues, moral or religious beliefs, principles, etc., that they do not actually possess . . . A person who feigns some desirable or publicly approved attitude, especially one whose private life, opinions, or statements belie their public statements."

How many times have you witnessed an agency president preach ethics only to cross the line to get a deal done? How many speeches have you heard about valuing employees only to lay them off when times get difficult? Peloton comes to mind. After marketplace competitors arose and times got tough, they quickly laid off 20% of their workforce. What about the CEO who leads the mandatory company-wide sexual harassment training, only to end up the biggest offender? Or what about work-life balance, but only for producers and high-level executives? What about diversity and inclusion? Leadership says that diversity is important, but they have taken zero steps to tackle the issue.

Authenticity Matters

Employees want authentic leadership, not the photoshopped, lip-service version of it. We live in a world of political division and mistrust of our leaders. We go through life suspect of everything. Groomed, airbrushed, and polished speeches aren't what employees want or need.

It's not enough for you to believe that you're authentic. Actions will win over belief every time. You must live it out both personally and professionally, whether in public or private, as failure to do so will negatively impact the perception of your authenticity. Once that is gone, it's difficult to earn back.

Authentic leaders understand the importance of surrounding themselves with honest feedback. They are aware of their strengths, weaknesses, and emotional triggers. Most times, showing the good, bad, and the ugly—as uncomfortable as it may be—is a far better option than pretending everything is fine. Like it or not, the people around you, including your employees, can already tell it isn't.

True authenticity will win your current employees' loyalty and trust and can attract top talent to your organization like—you guessed it—a magnet!

Integrity Matters

Imagine this: You're fighting the competition for a top account executive on your commercial lines team, so you slightly embellish your offering to a candidate and say what they want to hear. Perhaps you talk about being a "hands-off" manager who allows your team to work without micromanagement. Maybe you speak of flexibility for family time or bonus structure. Maybe you put a salary range on the job description but have zero intention of paying the salary at the top end of the spectrum.

Misrepresenting the job has long-term consequences and will result in your agency earning a reputation that's extremely hard to overcome. Unfortunately, setting high expectations and falling short on your promises is more often the rule and not the exception. In this job market, you can't afford to be in that spot. You can't be willing to pull an employee away from another organization based on what you perceive as a "little white lie" or material misrepresentation. Doing so will risk losing not only that person but others from your staff as soon as the broken commitment is discovered. Further, you now put your team in a challenging situation when that person quickly exits your agency, having them waste three months training someone only to have to repeat the process with someone else.

The talent war is brutal, and it won't get any easier if you misrepresent your available positions, company culture, or intentions. You need to be pure in your intentions, act with integrity, and find ways to recruit and attract that don't include things you aspire to versus what you currently offer. And again, with so many misrepresenting their offering, you need the credibility of employees both past and present to stress that what you offer is real. It's better to deliver on five out of five promises than seven out of fifteen.

Empathy

Empathy is tied to emotional intelligence and the ability to "recognize, reason with, and regulate emotions, both in oneself and others." As mentioned earlier, one of the reasons employees leave is due to failed leadership, specifically one that is not empathetic to the plight of their employees. How often do you ask someone how they are doing, they say, "Fine," and that's the end of the conversation? Further, how often have you masked your own emotions in the workplace because it would hurt the narrative that you have created for yourself?

I have many shortcomings, but my employees agree (I asked) that I deeply care about them, am empathetic to their challenges, am understanding of their mistakes, and will absolutely go to war to protect them. If anything has strengthened my talent magnet the most, I think it's this.

My relationship with my team members runs deep. I have a fairly good pulse on their family life, current events, and challenges. When the pandemic hit, I was acutely aware of each employee's specific challenges and put myself in their place before coming up with an action plan. And even before putting myself in their place, I probed to confirm that I truly had a grasp of the challenges each was having to go through. I made sure it was clear that I could never sympathize with their situation, as I hadn't lived it from their angle, but would do everything in my power to accommodate and adjust as if I was going through the same thing.

In the end, I don't have to promise things to my team. They know my yes means yes and my no means no. When candidates apply to work for me, they usually come from family, friends, or the friends of my employees. I don't need to pitch to them, do a dog and pony show, or promise them the world. I just have to keep doing what I'm doing. I'm not perfect, so I don't have the perfect work environment, but that just means there is room to grow. We have the basics in place: authenticity, integrity, and empathy. People aren't drawn to my agency because of outlandish salaries or a giant corporate ladder; they're drawn to us because we do the simple things right, every single day.

CHAPTER 14:
DO YOUR OPPOSITION RESEARCH

There are rich teams, and there are poor teams. Then there's fifty feet of crap. And then there is us.

—Billy Beane, Money Ball

Fighting the talent war will take significant research and planning. You must have a comprehensive understanding of your competitors, both local and abroad. That's no easy feat, and the abroad part sometimes feels next to impossible. That said, you have to spend hours studying the proverbial game film so that you can exploit the weaknesses of your competitors. And even if you identify the weakness, are you willing to provide prospective talent with something better than the agency down the street, in your state, or even across the country? How do you know if your mousetrap is better than theirs? You need to know whether you can compete for talent and how to do so, and to do that, you'll need intimate working knowledge of your competition.

An excellent place to start is knowing which agencies are in your backyard. You'll have to build a private database of agency intel. It sounds simple, but when was the last time you researched your competition? You may know about some of the agencies that are trying to steal your clients, but that could be just a fraction of the agencies in your area. For example, since my company insures artisan contractors, we have lots of competition. In fact, I would say that we have at least a hundred agencies in the southern California area that are actively trying to take our clients at any given time. So, I can't just rely on the information I gather anecdotally from clients. I need to dig deeper.

What data are you looking for from your competition, exactly? For starters, you want to know the following:

- Agency name
- Domain name
- Agency leadership

- List of current employees (can be obtained through LinkedIn or ZoomInfo)

  o Special Note: ZoomInfo also has most cell numbers, so it's a great way to connect with prospective candidates.

  o You can also pull the license info on employees to identify their time in the insurance business. This goes a long way in narrowing a talent search.

- List of former employees (LinkedIn Sales Navigator can help with this.)

- Mission Vision Values Statement

- Services provided to the client

- Locations (Are they near a freeway or is it more difficult to get to?)

- Benefits offered (Indeed, Zip Recruiter, and the agency's website will usually contain most of this info. The job postings on Indeed and Zip Recruiter also provide a list of benefits.)

- Niche focus

- Ownership model

A word of caution: You only have so much time. Many of the things I mention are tedious and time consuming. But fear not—you can outsource a lot to independent contractors on Fiverr or Upwork. However, I find that the more information you provide up front to the researcher dramatically improves the results.

Insurance association agency member lists are a great starting point. You can generally get a pretty good list of agencies with that alone. The great news is that they usually have a point of contact, including an email address. Having that information allows you to find their website and obtain a fair amount of the available information.

Google is another place to look. Quality agencies have learned by this point that they need lots of five-star reviews to remain relevant and have leveraged companies like Podium and Rocket Referrals to build their online presence. You might as well take advantage of the free resource. Because I am niche focused, I narrow my searches to those likely to insure contractors. I use a variety of search keywords like construction insurance, contractors' insurance, and artisan contractors' insurance so that I pick up as many local agencies as I can from both paid and organic listings.

As mentioned previously, Sales Navigator and ZoomInfo are great resources for building agency lists with employee data and contact information. ZoomInfo is expensive but worth it. However, if you're more budget conscious, you can obtain a lot of info from Sales Navigator for less than $50 a month. Once you've built your database to a high level, I strongly suggest you research the competition that is best equipped to poach your talent.

A key part of your research should focus on the regional or national agencies right in your backyard. One of the first questions agencies confront is whether they even have the capital to compete for seasoned A-players against the larger agencies. However, keep in mind that it isn't always about the money. Over the past thirty-six months, young professionals have clearly made it known that while better wages are important, they want to feel supported and protected. They want some flexibility, autonomy, and growth opportunities. So don't get discouraged just because you have several extremely large competitors in your area.

The next thing I would focus on in your research is the reputation of the competing agencies.

Pro Tip: Reach out to your major insurance company relationships. You would be surprised at how open underwriters can be. It isn't too difficult for underwriters to identify submission quality, demanding producers, or even if the competing agency is behind in leveraging technology. You can't ask this for every agency in your database, so I would reserve this tactic for your largest potential competitors.

It's important to remember that every agency lies on a spectrum in the industry. At one end, they're smaller, maybe suburban or rural, and community driven. On the opposite end, they're very large, very corporate, and rigidly structured—but may provide an opportunity to climb the corporate ladder. Either agency could be fast paced and entrepreneurial or more institutional in nature. Further, one agency could even be recognized as a talent farm, where new hires cut their teeth and move on, similar to the Enterprise Rental Car Companies Leadership Program (to use an example from another industry). You need to know where your agency fits on the spectrum.

Now that you've researched them, how do you compare to your competition? Do they offer better pay but have a revolving door of talent? High turnover for them could mean an opportunity for you. Are they mostly just providing living wage increases as opposed to performance-based compensation? With increasing inflation, this will become an Achilles heel for agencies. What about the general perception of the agency in the industry? I have competitors from whom I would never poach talent because their employees have been forced to compromise ethics for the sake of new business. Once you go down that road, it's difficult to find your way back. My competitors could use a lot of adjectives to describe me, but my business ethics are unquestionable.

To answer the questions mentioned above, you must have a deeper understanding of your competition's culture. You need to be able to identify whether the agency's behavior values producers more than the service staff, which is a frequent problem in this industry. When you stumble upon those situations, you've found gold—even if your compensation package can't match your competitor. You can't put a price on dignity! What about the agency's attitude toward education? Can you learn whether they provide long-term career paths and support it with mentoring and structured education programs? How does their culture handle conflict? Is there a middle-management level involved in the process, or does the owner get hands-on with staff issues? Do they pair great account managers with pain-in-the-ass producers because the account manager is the only one equipped to handle them? Or maybe account managers split duties between producers, each with their own way of doing things, which creates additional friction points in the daily workload.

Consider the social or community aspect of the agency. Do they have the flexibility for nonproducers to be able to attend family events? Can Janice, the account manager, leave for her son's baseball game in the early afternoon like Frank, the producer? Or does she have to rely on someone else to take him and hope to see a few video clips later? As an agency owner, I have been blessed to coach thirty-one seasons of youth sports and have missed maybe three games in the past decade. My team needs to have that opportunity; their family is just as important as mine. You better believe that I enforce the "you will not miss your kid's game" policy! Sadly, I am an outlier in that area.

Additionally, are there opportunities for team building and recognizing support staff along with producers? New production is often publicly celebrated and rewarded, while retention ratios driven by account managers are typically only addressed when there is a retention problem.

You'll only find out this information through significant time and effort. But fortunately, technology has made life a whole lot easier! For example, Glassdoor is a great resource for information on larger agencies. A word of caution, however: Pay close attention to both negative and positive reviews. Be careful to identify reviews written by agency leadership themselves—designed to make them look better—or reviews written by the "Karen" of the office who would never be happy no matter what. These are not accurate reflections of the agency. Unfortunately, if the agency is smaller, there are lower odds of getting a large enough sample size of reliable information. However, it's still worth a look.

Circling back to LinkedIn Sales Navigator, this tool will give you the capability to identify, through a simple search, employees in your area that have worked for a competing agency. The great thing about it is that you can narrow your search by the agency's employee count, the employee's title and duration with the company, and even their former employers. Your next step will be to connect by directly messaging them to see if they can chat about their current and past experiences. Even if they don't connect, they will still know that you viewed their profile and will likely take a look at yours. This is an indirect way to get their attention. There is also software that can automate the messaging process (just note that LinkedIn doesn't like them).

It isn't always easy to get LinkedIn connections to enter a dialog, so you need to think and act like a recruiter. Emphasize that you're trying to build long-term relationships along with being a resource. The best thing to do is be honest and transparent. Communicate your desire to continue building upon your best-in-class operations and benefits, as there's always something more that you could be doing to improve the culture of your organization. This type of messaging will resonate with both Millennials and Gen Z. In fact, if you message ten insurance professionals, eight will connect with you, and three will likely engage with you. You might be surprised by what they're willing to share with you. Take note: If they're sharing information, your employees are too. This simple information-gathering approach might just result in your agency finding a legitimate job candidate for the present and/or future. If you think they will be a longer-term play, it's crucial to develop a game plan for staying in touch.

Another option is to reach out to recruiters in your area for information. There are plenty of them, and they would be more than happy to share their insight, hoping to earn your business. Simply ask them about the competitors in your space and what benefits and compensation package is needed to compete against the other agencies. They will likely give you the requested information unless they have an existing contract with that firm. In that situation, simply move on to another recruiter. I recommend talking to multiple recruiters anyway to validate the information you've been provided. Hopefully, throughout your research process, you've been taking detailed notes and have a spreadsheet broken down by each category for quick reference later.

You should also begin following individual agencies on LinkedIn, Facebook, Instagram, and TikTok. You'll notice three things: 1) they will likely highlight some of their agency's fun events for employees, 2) their involvement efforts in the community, and 3) specific value-added services they are offering clients.

The next step in your research is to review the local job postings. I guarantee your competitors are all looking to hire within the next six months. About a year ago, we were searching for a new account manager, and there were sixty job postings for the same role in our immediate area alone. Take a look at each job posting and identify the most attractive parts of each one, including its phrasing. Is the offer compelling enough to convince someone to dive deeper and learn more about that agency? Identify any benefits they offer that you don't. Maybe they provide the same thing but describe it in a more attractive and engaging manner. Perhaps the job role is the same but comes with a better title? Titles are a big deal in the agency world. Are you able to identify something you can offer but didn't think to include?

The idea is to ethically research your competition and then use that information to compare it against your own value proposition. When your agency knows what the competition offers, it can determine whether changes are financially feasible.

If so, you can better prioritize where you can make the most impact and how to implement them. But at that point, you likely will need to circle back to your current employee benefits and provide the new ones to existing team members first. You want to make sure they can affirm that the comp plan and perks actually exist and communicate the difference these make for both the culture and the individual.

CHAPTER 15:
RECRUITMENT STRATEGIES

The secret of my success is that we have gone to exceptional lengths to hire the best people in the world.

—**Steve Jobs**

Before we dive into the specifics of recruitment strategies, it's important to remember that in the future, successful agencies will look for talent in places they never have before. The Great Resignation created waves of talent looking for another place to land. From Starbucks employees to other financial service employees, everyone is reevaluating where they want to build their career. You should also be targeting the following groups:

- Military spouses
- Transitioning stay-at-home parents
- Minority communities
- People with disabilities
- Older workers and members of AARP
- Out-of-state labor
- High school and community college students

Of course, there are the traditional routes as well. The point is to keep an open mind and develop a dynamic action plan.

Internship Programs

One traditional avenue of talent recruitment is an internship program. If it's done well, it can really work to your advantage. However, there's a lot of ambiguity about what a best-in-class internship program looks like.

If you consider implementing an internship program, it needs to be intentional and have a specific outcome in mind. Your program can't be like most, where the intern is stuck doing basic clerical work all day or left floundering to find something to do. Word gets out among college students about whether you have a great internship or a weak one. You should have an official internship roadmap that makes it clear from the interview process that the desired outcome of the program is to hire talented graduates.

As far as the process goes, I'm a firm believer in getting the intern licensed, which involves licensing classes for the first week (in person or online). Then I have them go through a practical training program like my second business, Total CSR, to learn the skills to contribute during their internship, which is another week and a half long.

This training will allow the intern to make a meaningful contribution to the organization for the remaining five and a half weeks, if you structure it like a typical eight-week internship program. Further, it demonstrates that you're committed to education and developing talent whether they ultimately become a part of your organization or not. Even if your agency doesn't offer them employment at the end of the program, they would be miles ahead of other new-to-industry candidates, which is a huge value—especially as you work to gear your agency brand toward the next generation. If, on the other hand, you want to make them an offer, they likely won't look for a job elsewhere in the industry because they'll already be connected and invested in your operations.

Highly structured internship programs like the one mentioned above allow agencies to vet individuals to determine whether they can learn. They also allow you to see their work ethic in action before bringing them on for a full-time opportunity. This is a cost-effective way to have potential job candidates self-eliminate from the future hiring process (because they can see the type of work they will be doing), which can save you months of time, effort, and compensation.

Things to consider before implementing an internship program:

- Have a designated team to oversee the program. The internship can't just be created by someone on an island. If you've ever interned at a company where the receptionist babysat you because the agency owner decided to have an intern on a whim, you'll know what I mean. Each team member will play a role in planning and delegating involvement from other relevant employees.

- Managers, senior-level leadership, or agency owners should be directly involved with the program. This involvement could be as simple as a welcome chat and maybe even a lunch. It's not tough to have one lunch over the course of an eight-week internship program. Remember, you are recruiting. You should take the time to emphasize the culture and "walk the walk" with integrity.

- You need to know your end goal. Do you want multiple interns going through the process hoping that one of three would be interested and take the job? Maybe you plan to offer them part-time work during the school year as a steppingstone to a full-time position upon graduation.

- I strongly recommend having a detailed calendar of what to expect for the eight weeks, including lunches, company events, and so on. You want to treat the intern as an employee. Give them every opportunity to interact with the team outside of the tasks you give them. The internship shouldn't feel like court-ordered community service, and you have to generate some excitement.

Social Media

Another recruiting tactic is strategic brand building on social media. Some platforms are better than others depending on your end goal, so consider carefully. A safe bet is LinkedIn, which is well known for professional networking, recruiting, and gathering information on career opportunities. If you consider recruiting here for current industry employees, purchase Sales Navigator now (if you ignored my suggestion to buy it during the database exercise in the previous chapter.)

Once you have completed your investigation into potential recruits, connect with them on LinkedIn and include a note to see whether they would be open to a conversation. I encourage doing this year-round. You need to be candid and say that you don't have a spot now, but you're growing rapidly, and it might be worth staying in touch.

Sound familiar? I'm being intentionally repetitive here in case you skipped over my previous LinkedIn pitch.

I also like sending direct messages to potential recruits before and after connecting with them. I might send a message saying, "I'm looking to find higher-level candidates like you, and I would love to know what you love most about your job, what the perks you can't live without are, and what type of things would make you not want to work there anymore." Again, you'll find that many are willing to provide you with that valuable information.

Since you should do this activity year-round, you need to consider designating someone in the agency to manage this task. It only takes a few minutes a day and is best done by someone in a leadership position. And please, don't be like the others spamming messages on LinkedIn. Take the time to review the profile and generate your message based on the details you discover.

I also recommend asking employees to connect with your new connections. As your agency posts about great things happening at your company, you'll have a better chance of a candidate seeing your content if more than one of you is connected. This also means more advocates potential employees could reach out to when researching your agency.

While LinkedIn is career oriented, you must also consider the trifecta of social media: Meta (Facebook), Instagram, and Tik Tok. These sites might give you a better snapshot of the agency's culture than what is portrayed on LinkedIn.

On Instagram and Facebook, I recommend creating a new account specifically for research. Like and follow the company page of the potential candidates you have connected with and then see what company posts they have and who is tagged or described in them. If you want to get really granular, you can look for patterns of likes and comments on pictures, which could help you further understand the depth of a given relationship. If you set this account up to monitor fifty agencies in your area, a team member could probably look through the past twelve months of post history for all of them in under one business day.

Tik Tok is relatively new to business promotion compared to

Facebook. You can connect with others, but the platform is geared toward video entertainment. That being said, several successful professionals in pretty much every industry have created a following by offering great information. Case in point, most Millennials and Gen Zers now get their news from Tik Tok. If you want to attract younger professionals, Tik Tok is the bar they hang out in.

Another strategy that can be used in tandem is to launch a podcast in which you interview insurance professionals in your specific region about their journey, the challenges they faced along the way, and their thoughts on the ideal insurance brokerage. Your guests should skew younger (less than forty years old). Almost everyone I have ever spoken with would love to be on a podcast. It doesn't matter how many listeners you have but rather that you get face time with a potential candidate. The interviewee (potential recruit) will likely share the episode as a LinkedIn post, which will undoubtedly be seen by additional insurance professionals. After the episode airs, follow up by asking for referrals for another great guest.

The key with a podcast like this is to keep it local so that you can leverage it for its proper intent. The great news is that podcasts today are easy to record and inexpensive to edit if you aren't able to do it on your own. You could go to Fiverr and, in just a few days, have all the components of the podcast ready to go, along with a podcast editor that won't charge you much to edit a full episode. If you build it right, you could record episodes each week, which will further build your pipeline of potential talent for future openings. For those that you really have an interest in, I strongly suggest checking in with them quarterly and maybe even taking them to lunch.

You should also consider a makeover of your corporate website and social media pages. You should have a page dedicated to the recruitment of candidates. It should include your agency's value proposition and current employee testimonials. It's also not that difficult to create YouTube testimonials from current employees that are accessible to potential candidates. This is an excellent way for candidates to get a better idea of your agency's culture, work environment, and leadership. Be sure to only put die-hard loyalists' testimonials online, as recruiters and others will likely go to your website and attempt to recruit them.

I suggest gathering testimonials from employees with multiple experience levels and highlighting your agency's training, career path benefits, and even their experiences with management. You can share these videos across social media to build your brand and immediately create a positive association. You should also provide a candidate FAQ page to be open and transparent about frequent questions. A more advanced tactic is to place a pixel on the recruitment page and run retargeting ads with testimonials from team members. YouTube video ads don't cost you anything for the first five seconds and are only three cents a view beyond that. You can limit the ads to only show on subject matter you approve of. Include your logo and agency name from the very start, so even if they don't watch past five seconds, they at least see the branding.

Job Boards

Job boards like Indeed, Career Builder, LinkedIn, Monster, and Zip Recruiter are also popular for reaching large numbers of job seekers. Before using job boards, you should talk to recruiters to get insight into your local market and review other job ads from agencies in the area. You want to do this so you can adjust and revamp your job postings so they are more compelling than your competition. If you aren't great at writing job postings that catch the eye, consider using a site like Fiverr to hire someone to write them for you. Notice how I keep repeating Fiverr? I think, at one time, I was their biggest customer. I'm not kidding!

Also, since job boards reach a broader audience, be sure to fully vet the people who apply. The wide reach is appealing because you'll likely get more applicants, but the quality of these applications might not be as good. I do advise you to look past college degrees, but don't relax all your standards. Remember that you're looking for someone who will be a good culture fit, have a growth mindset, and have the aptitude for the work. Best-in-class agencies will front-end screen with assessments (aptitude, emotional intelligence, personality) prior to interviewing. Too many agencies make the mistake of only doing assessments at the tail end of the process because they don't want to spend the money up front. The front-end assessments dramatically decrease the time to hire and remove confirmation bias from later in the interview process.

Employee Referral Programs

Perhaps the best way to recruit is to have an official employee referral program. Smartrecruiters.com reported that 82% of employers rated employee referrals as the best recruitment source. This strategy tends to fast-track the recruiting process, as the current employee provides much more information on the candidate up front.

Now, not all employee referral programs are created equal, so just like the internship program, you need to be intentional, and most importantly, you need employee buy-in for this one to work. Your program needs to run like a well-oiled machine to be successful, so be sure to:

- **Have a standardized process.** Employees need to know where to direct potential recruits and whether they should contact a specific person via email, phone, etc. Also, what information should employees provide to the hiring manager or recruiter, and what information about the agency would you like them to share with the candidate?

- **Communicate regularly.** It would be best to make sure employees are aware of the program. Even if you're not actively hiring, letting employees know that this exists will keep their eyes peeled for a good candidate that you may not want to let pass you by. Your team should be fully bought into the strategy of nurturing potential friends and colleagues for the long-term success of the agency.

- **Incentivize.** Consider offering recognition and compensation to those that participate and help make the program successful. Some companies offer a weekend getaway, some offer cash, and some hold events to show appreciation. What you choose to do should match your culture. Even setting up an interview while not in hiring mode should be rewarded.

If you have no other recruiting strategy, you need an employee referral program. The benefits substantially outweigh the costs. You have easier access to recruits since they are warm leads and personally vetted relationships, and you'll spend less money and time recruiting. Your employees help amplify your brand with the knowledge that their credibility is on the line. Employee recruits tend to stay on longer, and stats show a higher employee satisfaction rate.

Universities, Community Colleges, and Community Engagement

Another more traditional route is attending job fairs and utilizing job boards at universities and community colleges. The more you're involved and present in the community, the better. Connecting with the business admin programs and communication programs and engaging professors can pay big dividends. Professors have a desire to connect top-performing students with both intern and job opportunities, and many welcome business owners coming in to speak on different career paths.

I can't stress enough how important it is to go into low-income or minority communities and offer classes that aren't specifically insurance related. As I mentioned early in this book, they are going to be the long-term solution to our talent crisis. This educational experience could be anything from preparing resumes and interview strategies to financial management. The process is inexpensive and opens another avenue to introduce people to the wonderful world of insurance. Our industry has done such a terrible job making ourselves known to them and showing we care. With this strategy, you can establish trust within the community and ultimately build a pipeline of potential hires.

Advanced Coverage In-Person Seminars

Attending advanced insurance coverage seminars is another great tactic. Top talent wants to learn and is motivated to do so. Historically, you receive a list of people in attendance, but you can also discretely take pictures of their placards and make the rounds. (I suggest doing this at lunch when everyone is away.) The networking there has always been great for our agency. In the past, I've identified the local, California-based talent and made it a point to connect. I offer value with advice on technology, process improvement, and even talent management. Even if this does not lead to a direct candidate, it continues to build our brand.

Association Events and Conferences

Insurance association events and insurance conferences also present a great opportunity to network and get in front of a captive audience. Several times a year, I speak at the agency management conferences where I will have anywhere between fifty and three hundred people attending my session. This approach provides insight into how I run my agency and who I am as a person, which yields additional discussions with potential candidates. These discussions help build rapport and attract talent into my agency organically. Believe it or not, it's actually not that difficult to become a speaker. Once you perform well, they look forward to having you speak each year. When I'm not doing this, I leverage the conference apps and direct message those in my area with an offer to connect, even for a few minutes. As a reminder, this doesn't have to be you doing it, but it should be a team member involved in some level of leadership. That's why it's great to always bring back-up to conferences.

Professional Recruiters

And, of course, there are professional recruiters. I reserve this for top-level talent or if I'm struggling to find a niche specialist. It costs anywhere from 15 to 20% of the first year of your new hire's compensation, so you want to make sure it's worth it. However, not all professional recruiters are considered equal. If you go this route, make sure the recruiter you work with clearly understands what you're looking for and is not just trying to place a warm body. Unfortunately, many recruiters farm job boards for resumés and don't spend quality time learning about your needs or the candidates they offer you.

Also, find a recruiter who's familiar with your specific niche or is at least willing to spend the time to get a proper grasp of your needs. My preference is to work with recruiters who bill me by the hour. As a rule, I pay for work performed, not lucky guesses. In exchange, I'm willing to pay a higher hourly rate that compensates according to the value provided.

The Bottom Line

Recruitment needs to be a year-round effort. Sometimes you're just building relationships in preparation for when you have an opening. For this reason, you need to have a system and clearly defined process in place. It needs to run like clockwork, so tasks don't fall to the wayside when things are busy. Recruiting needs to be a part of your daily construct.

The benefit of having an ongoing recruiting strategy is that you continue to build your network. So even if a contact isn't interested in coming over to your agency, they likely know somebody who would. Further, you may have a candidate that turned your offer down a few months ago or even two years ago, but perhaps today they feel differently, or their circumstances have changed. Continue to network with and review those past candidates on a regular basis. To put it in context, just because a producer does not earn the client's business one year doesn't mean that they shouldn't continue to pursue a great opportunity.

And one last thought: Let's assume you have too many candidates for your needs. This situation is rare in the marketplace, but it does happen. You can refer that person to other agencies in the area. The insurance community is small, and you never know when you'll need a favor. I've also found it to be a great way to deter them from stealing one of your clients. If they feel like they already owe you, they're far more likely to tell a producer to back off.

CHAPTER 16:
ONBOARDING

At Google, we front-load our people investment. This means the majority of our time and money spent on people is invested in attracting, assessing, and cultivating new hires.

—Laszlo Bock

If you feel your onboarding process is haphazard or outdated, you're not alone. In our industry, onboarding hasn't improved much in thirty years. In fact, there is strong evidence that it has gone backward. We essentially bring someone in, have HR go through the paperwork with them, and then sit that person at a desk. We give them a few hours of explanation on the systems and a brief walk around to make introductions throughout the office, and then we set them loose to learn with a trial by fire method. And if they're really lucky, they might shadow another account manager for a week. Hardly a way to set them up for success.

Onboarding is an opportunity to create a story—a story about your organizational culture, process, systems, values, and mission. High-quality onboarding is also critical for building your talent magnet and retaining your employees. A poorly executed process is a disservice to both the people we bring on and our business. Those first impressions create a lasting impact and set the direction of each employee's career with your agency and your company's reputation as a desirable (or not!) place to work.

That new hire is hopeful for the future and excited to start a new job, maybe a new career. Further, your new hire's friends (inside and outside the industry) will immediately ask what their new job is like. This moment may be the only time they'll discuss their employer with their friends and business associates (other than to gripe). So, it's critical to make a great first impression, build the brand, and tell a story you'd be happy for your employees to share. I am going to do another deep dive here as our industry is generally pretty terrible at this. Buckle up.

Create an Epic Onboarding Experience

Your welcome and orientation experience are one of the keys to happy, productive, long-term employees. Remember, your onboarding process will also be a billboard advertisement in your talent magnet. Think about what makes your team or the new hire's role unique and find a way for your onboarding to stand out.

To start, you should have a clear owner of the welcome and orientation experience. Is it the account manager or an HR representative that will walk the new hire through the office? Who will show them where the kitchen is located, where the coffee machine is (and how to work it), and where the bathroom is? Will there be a "hand-off" to a buddy? If you can script a sales call, you can script a system for an appointed company ambassador.

Think about what the process looks like. It should start from the top and roll down. The agency president or senior leadership should reach out to the new hire every two or three days until their start date. It would also be helpful for the buddy to reach out ahead of time and even offer to grab coffee or lunch during the onboarding. Perhaps consider including the three top leaders whom the new hire will interact with when planning your coffee or lunch. If schedules allow it, top leadership, team lead, and a buddy can meet to give the new hire a warm welcome so their first day isn't going in cold. They can go in and find familiar faces.

If the new hire has a dedicated workstation, make them feel special and let the team decorate the space. If you're hot desking or working remote, maybe think of how you can create a fun, travel-sized welcome kit to get them started. Hot desking might be unfamiliar for many, so creating a caddy filled with treats might help normalize the experience. Whether working in-house or remotely, you can deliver a branded care package to your new hire as soon as they sign the employment agreement to show that you care, that you are excited for them to start, and that this will be a positive working experience.

You should always expect their previous employer to try to retain your new hire. So, the sooner you send a message and care package, the better. It could include an agency coffee mug, T-shirt, cool gadgets, baked goods, or any other treat you can think of. Believe it or not, they may feel guilty about going back to their previous employer if they have received this care package from you. It's the principle of reciprocity.

If you believe onboarding doesn't matter, think again! Here are some recent statistics reported by SaplingHR.com:

- Great onboarding can improve employee retention by 82% and productivity by 70%.

- Only 12% of employees surveyed felt their company did a good job at onboarding.

- 70% of those surveyed who had a good onboarding experience believed they had the "best possible job."

- Employees who had a negative onboarding experience are twice as likely to look for other career opportunities.

- 20% of new hires are unlikely to recommend an employer to a friend if they had a negative onboarding experience.

According to Click Boarding, an employee onboarding software company, 69% of employees are more likely to stay with a company for three years if they experience great onboarding. Think back to your own experience working at a company with either really great or terrible onboarding. Didn't that experience affect your overall impression of the company and set the tone for the rest of your employment there? Before I get on my high horse, let me confess that I don't have a perfect track record of doing this properly. But I've learned from my mistakes, and with each new hire, I try and improve upon the experience. In short, I have failed my way into success. It's better if you skip the failure and go right to success.

So, you're convinced that onboarding needs to be a part of your systems and processes for your talent magnet. But how do you go about creating an onboarding process that benefits your new talent, your recruiting strategy, and your business—without falling back to the old ways?

Preparation is the key. If you put a well-organized process in place, you can run it on repeat. Start with organizing employee resources both within the company and for the local or immediate area. Get all their resources set up before their first day. It sounds simple, but you'd be surprised how many important details get missed. One of the biggest is making sure your new employee has a computer, desk, chair, and access to programs. Provide resources that will make their job and life around work easier! Consider the following:

- **Security logins and access keys.** We sometimes wait to set up logins and access keys. There is nothing that says, "you aren't part of the team yet," like welcoming a new hire with locked doors.

- **Desk (and chair).** Ergonomics matter. I have team members that prefer to sit, some that prefer to stand, and even some that sit cross-legged. You must provide a setup that gets the best performance out of them.

- **Computer.** If you're replacing an employee, has the computer been wiped clean? Does it look like they're getting hand-me-downs, or are they walking into a functional operating system that's been set up specifically for them? I even suggest setting up favorite pages on their web browser. Speaking of web browsers, many insurance companies continue to require Microsoft Internet Explorer, despite the fact that it's no longer being updated. Let them have favorites pages both for Internet Explorer and Google. Why make them reinvent the wheel when they don't have to?

- **Monitors, cables, and pesky adapters.** You should have an inventory list of every item they need, down to the mouse, keyboard, cords, and adapters. Also, make sure to ask about their preference of mouse as everyone tends to have a preferred style. And always provide a new keyboard. Nothing is worse than showing up to a keyboard covered in the previous user's crumbs. If you give equipment to a new hire, and it isn't set up, they will more than likely set off hunting for the missing pieces. The best practice is to have the desk, chair, and other equipment up and running.

- **Logins for hardware, password management tools, role-specific software, and apps.** It seems obvious. Yet again, I bet you can name at least one time when you started a job and had to wait for or ask for login information. For example, you can get into the software system but haven't been given the access code to the copier. This also applies to time and attendance tools for HR purposes!

- **List of local amenities.** If employees know where to find the best lunch spots, gas stations, stores, and the like, it will help them acclimate to your office and area more quickly. Providing this list can show you value their time away from work. This might not apply if you're onboarding a remote worker, but that's an entirely different book (Agency Amplified).

- **Specialist tools and equipment.** Consider whether you have any tools and equipment, such as scanners or a binding machine, which could be unfamiliar or infrequently used. You have them for a reason, so introduce them before they're needed. You want to create "wow" experiences for clients and employees alike.

Get Paperwork Started

Paperwork is the most boring, confusing, and frustrating part of the onboarding process. So much can be held up by a missing signature on one piece of paper or an illegible bank number. Get your paperwork out of the way as soon as possible. The faster you finish it off, the quicker you can focus on the engagement side of onboarding. Electronic acceptance is a simple workaround to speed up the paperwork time, as it removes the delays of postage, filing, and manual data entry. Not only will it significantly speed up your time to hire, but you'll create an epic first impression with your new hires. You should complete these essential documents before a new hire's first day:

- Employment contract

- Any customized forms for ordering equipment, uniforms, "get to know me," etc.

- Policies that require acknowledgment

- Payroll, banking, and tax forms

- VISA & work requirements

- Health insurance enrollment

Paperwork is a brain drain. You don't want your new hire to feel exhausted on day one. On the contrary, you want them to leave the first day exhilarated and ready to return the next day. If the paperwork is done before your new hire starts, their first day can focus on integrating with the team and acclimating to your culture, systems, and processes. You can create a more memorable first day when the mechanics are out of the way. Another benefit is that the sooner you get them entrenched in your system prior to their first day, the less likely they are to backtrack for another offer at the last moment. I prefer to ask the candidate what will happen if their employer offers to match or improve upon our job offer. I then go into my speech about employers who only offer raises once someone else is interested. That's not showing the employee they are valued; it's showing that they are necessary. Those are two very different things.

Get Others Involved

Beyond HR, other employees, teams, and departments should also be involved in the onboarding process. These other groups have a significant impact on a new hire's engagement. For example, the Operations Manager or Commercial Lines Manager may be an employee's key point of contact. Still, it's likely that they will also benefit from access to IT, the claims department, and accounting.

For this reason, all agency leaders must have proper access and transparency regarding the onboarding process, along with a clear outline of their tasks. 61% of best-in-class onboarding businesses give their managers visibility into the status of new hires. If managers understand what employee onboarding is about, the effects it can have on engagement, and the positive effect it will have on staff retention, they'll be more than happy to do their part. That said, I also suggest making it easier for them to contribute by automating certain tasks.

Communication is essential and one of the most manageable tasks to customize and automate for an onboarding system and managers. Correspondence from the team leader is critical—even before day one. From the time the employment contract is signed, new employees must begin building a rapport with their manager. The process doesn't have to be complicated. Consider this simple road map to follow before day one.

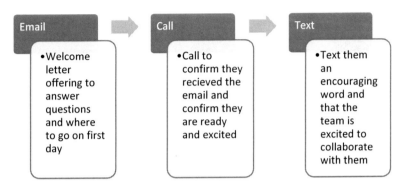

Email	Call	Text
•Welcome letter offering to answer questions and where to go on first day	•Call to confirm they recieved the email and confirm they are ready and excited	•Text them an encouraging word and that the team is excited to collaborate with them

Multiple layers of management should be involved in the onboarding process. A team lead could simply send a welcome email or text and make a quick call to a new hire. The operations manager could also do the same. At the same time, I encourage all employees to connect with the new hire on LinkedIn and send them a welcome message within forty-eight hours after hiring. The point is to get the team leaders' team members involved so that the new hire comes in warm.

Share Valuable Information

People want to join organizations that align with their values and beliefs. It's important to keep reinforcing your culture, brand, and unique style to new hires before day one. Don't overwhelm them but share information that will leave an impact from the start. Here's a list of the must-have onboarding activities to help them feel ready for their first day:

- **CEO welcome.** The more you customize this and make it personal to the new hire, the better. Perhaps they recently moved to the area, adopted a pet, or graduated from college. Add a personal, heartfelt touch. Canned

CEO welcomes are not as impressive.

- **Company vision, values, and history.** Make a connection between how the new hire fits into the story and how they can further the vision.

- **Team introduction.** Who's who in the zoo! Consider introductions that show professional highlights and include personal insight. For example, instead of introducing Jim as the highest-producing guy that's been with the company for fifteen years, add personal details. Jim likes fishing and is the go-to for fantasy football. He has a dog named Loki and a wife of twenty-five years. This exercise gives new hires a starting point to enter conversations more easily. And if you're really on top of things, I suggest sharing insights from their personality profile or even enneagram. This will greatly reduce communication issues and misunderstandings.

- **Team lingo and terminology.** Every company has at least one acronym that anyone outside the group wouldn't get. Be sure to share a few right out the gate, if you have any. Otherwise, they might hear "SOP" (standard operating procedures) and have no idea what it means. If they're brand new to the industry, even more lingo needs to be communicated and defined. Everything from the difference between producers and account managers to terms like ex-dates and currently valued loss runs.

- **Invite new hires to Slack or Teams.** You should also provide the agency ground rules for use. Our team is a bit more laid back, and it's not uncommon for more than a few memes to be used throughout the day.

- **Team rituals and ceremonies.** Help your new hire to understand what to expect with the recurring activities that make working there predictable and, hopefully, fun. When are your weekly team meetings, or do you provide regular team lunches? Do you have a "rally cry" or dress down Fridays?

- **First-day schedule (and probably first week and month schedule).** Give your new hire something to work for or refer to. New hires will wonder whether they are on target, so give them the target.

The First Day

Walking into a new office can be daunting. Even the most capable new hire faces the fear of the unknown. They also feel overwhelmed by information and new faces. Ensuring the new hire has an idea of their first day's agenda and orientation process before they arrive on day one is crucial.

Information should be drip-fed if it's to be retained in any meaningful way. Day one is all about the agenda and orientation. Focus on the welcome experience and explain the team ceremonies and rituals. Remember the welcome email, call, and text roadmap? This is an excellent tool for dripping information to a new hire. The first email or text can be the "expect more emails or texts on what comes next." Then send a text or email about the day one agenda and orientation.

You could send a text or email asking how they felt after their first day. Find out if they have any questions or things that could be improved on for the next person. It's important to demonstrate that you value their input from the start. You should also include a reminder about the next few days to come and what to expect. And remember, this talent war we are facing has led to new hires leaving for other opportunities after just one week at an agency so it's best to solidify that relationship before their start date and double down on it within the first five days.

Assign a Buddy

Have you ever started a job and felt alone, not sure who to turn to, and as though you were inconveniencing teammates with a ton of questions? Consider assigning a support buddy to a new hire rather than a direct manager as their initial resource. They'll feel more comfortable asking mundane but essential questions about the office, culture, and quirks of the team. The buddy is also a great person to introduce the new employee around and tour the office to build rapport and relationships. You want a person with a mix of being social and embodying the company's values and work ethic.

It's important to consider whom you assign as a buddy. You don't want to force the position on an unwilling participant. Depending on your culture and team, you may rotate the buddy position or have one person that is the permanent buddy for the office. Consider whether you need to incentivize the buddy process. After all, it can be more work depending on how well your systems and processes are implemented during onboarding. But more than likely your ideal buddy has already come to mind.

Demonstrate and Communicate Your Company Values

Onboarding is a great way to give employees a more meaningful introduction to the workplace culture. Before day one, you would have laid the foundation. Now, it's time to walk the walk. You do this by giving the new employee meaningful time with critical leaders or influencers across the business. You reinforce your mission, values, and culture. New hires get to experience each within the context of daily operations.

Have your leaders communicate the company's values in their time with the new hire. If you've already got an incredible workplace culture, it will show, and the new hire will be able to envision their place in the organization. Both you and the new hire will solidify that they're the right fit for the organization.

Only 32% of organizations communicate their core values to candidates and new employees, leading to higher turnover (especially in the first three months). If you hire someone that has a shared set of values, they're going to need to see evidence of that from the start. I hate to beat a dead horse, but they will tell their friends about the level of attention and care they received.

The truth is that 99% of agencies only do a fraction of these things. Some may do a couple of them, but even those activities are often not executed well. If you do most of the above and do it well, you'll dramatically increase the chance of retaining that employee. These onboarding activities are an indirect way of building your talent magnet and pipeline. With the talent pool so limited, we can't afford to be wrong about someone or lose them simply because we failed to provide the onboarding experience they deserve. And trust me, when you do it effectively, word will spread fast.

CHAPTER 17:
TRAINING

Tell me and I forget, teach me and I may remember, involve me and I learn.

—Benjamin Franklin

Much like onboarding, agencies suck at training. In our industry, training has historically been reactive, an afterthought, or downright nonexistent. It wasn't handled through a defined process or system but rather on the "as needed" spectrum and mostly through job shadowing. We've talked about the importance of training and using it to attract top talent. However, we need to connect why training is crucial to our brand with how to implement it in a meaningful way.

Training is yet another indirect way to build your brand and become a talent magnet. Intentionally incorporating an engaging and valuable training experience into your agency is not just good business sense, it's also a brand builder. If people think of your agency as a great place to work and learn that invests in its people, that brand image will spread among existing staff, their associates, new-to-industry hires, and their friends who may have never even heard of an insurance career.

Of course, even if you become one of the top places to work thanks to your training program, you'll still lose a portion of employees to poaching—but at least they were great while you had them! There's still some good news though. When employees who leave end up at other agencies, the story of your training program will spread throughout those other organizations as well, further solidifying your brand and planting seeds for future recruitment.

The Training Evolution

So, to begin, we need to evaluate the way we used to or continue to do training. Traditionally, training fit into two buckets:

insurance coverage and insurance processes. We viewed it as rote memorization of coverage and maybe a small amount of haphazard roleplay. Maybe we offered some cross-selling training in the mix, but again, our efforts were more reactive than proactive.

Training then evolved to include technology and specific systems training. If you're old enough to remember filling forms in triplicate, using fax machines, and having pagers, you remember the learning curve of going from a typewriter to a word processor to ultimately transitioning to the PC and needing to figure out how to use email and cell phones. (If you're wondering, I'm talking about my dad's generation.)

Given the changing needs of the newest generation of employees, we also need to add soft skills to the equation. To be competitive, our employees need to have critical thinking and teamwork skills. They need to learn how to manage their time, communicate more effectively, and master the art of active listening—not to mention conflict management. If you aren't training them in these essential soft skills, you're opening the door for them to be poached by someone who will. Or worse yet, they'll stay with you and end up creating chaos for your culture.

The Four Buckets

Clearly, agencies can no longer rely on the two original training categories. We need to break down training into four buckets: process, coverage knowledge, technology and systems, and soft skills. And even if you or someone on your leadership team is very knowledgeable in all these areas, that doesn't mean you (or they) have the ability or time to teach others.

Effective teaching is a mix of skill and art. You need to understand different learning styles, generational nuance, and different ways to communicate information so that it's retained. Most agencies don't have someone in-house with the skillset for teaching, and thus need to outsource training—with good reason. There is so much to cover, and it requires great teachers to train effectively.

It isn't enough to just have the training buckets. Having a great teacher and a high-quality training process is crucial for each bucket's material to sink in and for your new hire to become successful beyond their training. Remember, this is a critical need of the new generation. In their minds, it's not optional.

Process Training

When everyone has their own way of doing things, it can be confusing for the new hire, and friction develops. The new hire will struggle to do things correctly and will likely be reprimanded for doing something improperly when they were just doing it the way they were taught. You want new hires to be raving about their onboarding and training experience, not end their days frustrated. A uniform system of processes is vital. New-to-industry hires that stay with your agency will end up training subsequent hires, and if there's no consistency, an unfortunate game of telephone starts. Each iteration gets progressively further from the original if not standardized from the start. From a recruiting perspective, there's also the chance that new team members will grab lunch with former coworkers and discuss how much easier life is with consistent processes across the board. You want those former coworkers to be envious of your team member and start inquiring about opportunities with your agency.

The first step in building a process training experience is to make sure team members are all doing things the same way. And not just with general topics but specific to each step of the process, including how you complete ACORD forms, label documents, and set timeframes for follow-up. For example, my agency has thirty-five specific processes, and everyone does them the exact same way. We didn't use to be like this, but we were deliberate in solving that problem. Here are eight steps to ensuring all your processes are aligned, which is simple conceptually but difficult to execute because it's tedious and boring:

1. Require every agency employee to list each job process they can think of.

2. Assign someone to compile the list and eliminate duplicates.

3. Present the list to your entire team and verify that all processes have been addressed.

4. Store the processes on a shared drive that's accessible to all employees.

5. Assign one process per week to each employee and have them write out step-by-step instructions.

6. Meet the following week to compare each employee's process and develop a best-practice process.

7. Designate one employee to transcribe the final version.

8. Record a video of each process so that learners have a

written description and a video version. The current generation is very video oriented, so this is extremely beneficial for new hires.

Once this is in place, you can assign the new hire to watch each video three times (which seems to be the most effective number) and then quiz them on the steps of the process to ensure they were paying attention. Next, have another employee walk them through the process on an existing account. A bit like job shadowing on a process. This activity allows the new hire to see any nuances that the video might not communicate. Last, have the new hire watch the video one more time to solidify what they learned. The new employee should usually be able to tackle the role on their own after this.

So why do you need to go through this in such specific detail? This training process makes new hires more successful right out of the gate, reduces friction points with the current staff, and improves retention. Due to poor onboarding and training, about 20% of new hires quit within the first forty-five days. This system helps mitigate that.

Coverage Knowledge

If you're new to the industry, the first step is to get licensed. Typically, this includes a fifty-two-hour licensing course. Very little of this pertains to understanding the business, but it's a necessary evil. In fact, I advise every new employee to forget whatever they have learned in the licensing course. They need relevant coverage knowledge from the start that, unfortunately, was historically gained by the sink-or-swim method. Hopefully, you can't relate to this, but I bet you can.

We should really teach coverage knowledge at multiple levels. Just like learning baseball, consider the basics first (T-ball), then the move to intermediate knowledge (high school baseball), and finally advanced knowledge (the major leagues). You can't expect a new industry hire to grasp intermediate or advanced concepts without a strong foundation.

While agency staff shouldn't be tasked with the heavy lifting of training, they are essential for relaying some aspects of coverage knowledge. Mentors with more coverage knowledge should help those with less, even if they're only two years ahead of the person they're mentoring. Do you have designated team members who will provide guidance when needed? These individuals should be available to regularly roleplay with others, so your team can become more comfortable explaining coverage in layperson's terms.

Also, consider your education policy, whether you have one or will implement one. Do you offer education reimbursement? Is it only if the person passes the course? Do you allow for in-person as well as online training? Is there a limit to how much education an employee can get each year? Are employees expected to do this during their free time or working hours? Is there a preferred educational roadmap of designations or specific coverage competencies? Of course, this isn't limited to coverage knowledge. You should consider an education policy for each bucket of training. However, since the options for coverage training are so vast and complex, it's important to have a specified roadmap set out in writing for employees to reference.

Technology and Systems Training

This partly ties into process training but also includes how to best leverage emerging tech and access relevant information on the platforms. For example, almost every agency is dealing with at least five insurance company online rating platforms. They all have different interfaces with different levels of sophistication. Employees shouldn't assume that they can find relevant information in the same place for every insurance company or even that the insurance company offers access to the same types of documents. So, part of the process training bleeds over to training in tech and systems outside of internal processes.

You might be tempted to think that an existing employee would have the motivation to research how to use the system properly. Still, many people are intimidated by emerging Insurtech and need some guidance along the way. This sentiment goes back to the culture you want to build. Ensuring each new hire is trained on the tech the agency uses will demonstrate that leveraging technology, learning new skills, and being open-minded to change (growth mindset!) is critical to success. This emphasis on tech training can work to change the minds of those who have a negative perception of insurance agencies and how outdated their technology may be. And again, they will share these new perceptions with their friends and business associates.

Soft Skills

Gen Z and Millennials want to know that you're willing to invest in them as people, not just as employees. While soft skill development helps on the business front, it can also improve their personal lives. Imagine if your friends notice you've suddenly become a better listener, improved the way handle conflict, or reduced your social anxiety reduced when going out. They're going to want to know why.

If you see a recurring theme here, it's that training not only reduces turnover and friction, but the positive effects will also spread to relationships outside of the organization. This will influence your organization's brand image as well as the image of our whole industry. A friend may point out that they noticed these changes and ask where their friend picked up the skills on how to resolve conflict or reduce their social anxiety and where they could get that training. Their answer will be "at work." That's you! They might end up engaging in an entire conversation around your agency, the culture, and management style and, if you're lucky, an inquiry about insurance career opportunities.

From an internal business perspective, soft skills, understanding generational differences, and communication styles will help new hires better communicate with team members and clients. Hopefully, the older team members will have completed this training, improved their communication, and built a better culture within the agency, especially as the younger generation begins to hone their skill set.

It's not hard to see why a great training program is essential for building a successful talent magnet. Again, it's simple but difficult. It's not something you can create within thirty days, and it requires buy-in from all team members. But doing it right will have a powerful impact on your culture and result in an even stronger talent magnet.

CHAPTER 18:
EMPLOYEE RETENTION

Initiate the preservation process when the person is still in love with the place not when they are fed up and ready to leave.

—Unknown

Employee retention is a critical component of your talent magnet. Each employee that departs your organization dampens the magnet's effect. High turnover disrupts the agency culture and sends a clear message to potential applicants that the work environment is less than desirable.

Employee turnover is also costly. Employee Benefits News reported that in 2017, employers spent an average of 33% of a worker's annual salary to replace just one employee. Last year, Terra Staffing Group put that in perspective, saying, "It will cost $12,000 to replace an entry-level employee making $36,000 a year." To replace a manager making $60K a year would cost $20K, and to replace an executive making $150K a year would cost $50K.

If you're wondering why they leave, you really don't have to look much further than management. Of course, culture, pay, and benefits matter, but employees typically don't quit a company—they quit a boss.

One of the biggest challenges I see in our space is that most agencies are flat organizations. The account manager and producer role usually report directly to the agency president. The agency president is often actively selling, so their time to manage the operation is limited. Let's be honest, most agency presidents and managers do very little managing. Many wouldn't even know how to do the processes their team members complete. On most days, they may go to a couple of staff members with a question about a specific account, but there's very little engagement beyond that. Even with larger organizations that have middle management, the challenge is that most in that position don't have the slightest clue how to manage, mentor, and lead their direct reports.

This chapter will talk about some concrete strategies for employee retention that fit the recurring theme of this book: things that are simple but difficult to do consistently. Additionally, we will identify ways to engage more frequently and at a deeper level that ultimately improves employee retention. After poor management, the next attributable reason for turnover is the quality of relationships at work. In short, do employees have friends within the workplace? Another challenge is the flexibility required to ensure a balanced home life. Next in line is the compensation and benefits package. I will now dive into each, and if you follow the steps I outline, it will dramatically shift the culture in the office, improve retention, and ultimately strengthen your talent magnet.

Purposeful Management Interactions for Employee Retention

Daily

Make a point to stop over and say hello to each team member every day. I prefer to do this at different times of the day, so I don't catch them all at once. The quiet ones will likely be in the background, hoping you would ask about them but never speaking up. I like to make these conversations unrelated to work, maybe asking about their kids or talking about some funny thing that happened. This activity is simply a connection point that shows you care about them for more than their work product. If you have seven direct reports, this will take you twenty to thirty minutes tops for an entire week of small talk. Not much to ask.

Weekly

Hold a weekly team meeting (and prepare an agenda). Attendance should be nonnegotiable. I like to start each session with a few minutes of learning, whether we talk about a coverage issue or a new insurance company market. Work through the agenda and then spend the last few minutes of the meeting focusing on two things:

- Problems and solutions that came up over the past week, so everyone can learn without having to experience the same issue with an underwriter or client.

- A "win or learn" portion where the account managers can share a success from the week and a failure or bonehead mistake. It takes time to develop the trust to be that open, but it demonstrates that the agency understands that mistakes happen. If employees feel free to share and learn from mistakes, they will have less anxiety and will likely come to management immediately when there is a problem.

Once a week, you should also check in with one of each team member's larger accounts. Quickly look in the agency management system and then ask a question like "How is the renewal going?" or "Did this issue get solved?" To close out the conversation, you can say, "Is there anything I can do to help?" 95% of the time, you'll hear no. Imagine how a team member would feel about management after hearing that you're willing to help every week for fifty-two weeks straight.

Monthly

Every month, have a one-on-one meeting with each of your direct reports. These meetings are usually twenty minutes or less. First, ask how the employee is doing. Next, focus on showing them appreciation. You should be able to identify at least one big win for the month or something they've done to improve office culture. The important part is to connect the action with the impact and express its value.

Sometimes you have troublesome employees, and it's more challenging to find something positive, but it's worth the effort. And if you can't find something positive to say about them over a couple-month window, they need to find a new agency.

Once that portion of the meeting is done, pivot to any performance issues and see how you might help them eliminate the problem.

The next part of the meeting is to bring up any ongoing issues that are frustrating them. This allows the team member to blow off a little steam to you, not the five other people sitting around them. As a rule, I don't tolerate triangulation. If someone has a problem, they need to bring it to me directly. The same should apply to your agency. This only works if you keep things confidential and listen without becoming defensive. If it's something that you could correct, simply check in the next month to see if progress has been made. And sometimes, there's nothing that can be done about the issue, and that needs to be clearly communicated as well.

The last part of the meeting is for asking whether the employee wants to know about the company, its direction, or more. This step allows them to feel in the know and more connected to the vision. You would be surprised how valuable this is.

If you do all this for each team member, it will require no more than seven to eight hours a month, and the effects will be transformative for your agency.

My challenge to you is to jot down the revenue size of each account manager's book of business, average account size, and the number of clients before and after you implement these tips. I have no doubt that your client retention rate will increase 2 to 3%, if not more, just by executing the above strategies. However, the real value is employee retention and solidifying relationships with your team members, which strengthens company culture, improves your organization's reputation and brand image, and results in a full-blown talent magnet.

Annual Reviews and Employee Retention

Annual reviews should be consistent and thoughtful. However, if you aren't executing weekly and monthly check-ins, consider doing quarterly reviews. Annual reviews could be too far apart if you aren't doing regular check-ins. You want these reviews to be intentional and productive.

The employee has spent the past twelve months working for you, and this is their report card. Treat it as such but with the additional sensitivity blended with candor to ensure a positive outcome. The employee should know where they're doing great and which areas need improvement. This meeting is also the time to revisit their career aspirations and let them hear you recommit to helping them along the way. Reviews are meant to visit company expectations, strengths, and weaknesses, chart a course for the future, and modify behaviors. However, this is also the best opportunity to convey the message that you care about your employee and want to learn more about them including:

- Goals for the future (yours and theirs)

- Successes over the past year

- Development, training, and growth

- The hurdle you can help them overcome

- What you can do to improve or support their success

Choose your words carefully, *listen*, and ask meaningful questions. For example, if you have a producer who seems to be faltering, it's better to start with questions like "how are you doing" and "how can I help" than to highlight low-performance metrics. If production is down, find out why and how to help before highlighting the possible internal struggle. I promise you that they are typically aware of the performance issue. Maybe they have a sick family member or are going through a separation. The point is to ask and listen instead of direct and dictate. Some people will open up as soon as you ask them, but others will hold on to their struggles and consider themselves very private people. In that case, it comes down to whether your employee trusts you to react well and/or keep their confidentiality. Be sensitive to this, especially with your newer employees, as they probably came from a place where they had troubles with management (recall that most people leave a job due to poor leadership), and it can be hard to transition to a new, safer space.

Consider incorporating the "stay interview" when you have your annual reviews. A stay interview is held to dig into why an employee chooses to stay with the company and what would cause them to leave. SHRM.org recommends asking some of the following questions:

- What do you look forward to when you come to work each day?

- What do you like most or least about working here?

- What keeps you working here?

- If you could change something about your job, what would that be?

- What would make your job more satisfying?

- How do you like to be recognized?

- What talents are not being used in your current role?

- What would you like to learn here?

- What motivates (or demotivates) you?

- What can I do to best support you?

- What can I do more of or less of as your manager?

- What might tempt you to leave?

Gather their responses and ensure you have a clear picture of what your employee considers important, how likely they are to stay with your company long term, and whether there is anything you can change or emphasize to ensure that they stay with your company and inspire others to join.

Friendships at Work

It's no secret that employees need to feel connected to their coworkers, and when they are, they report higher satisfaction at work. In 1999, Gallup reported that employees who have a best friend at work are:

- 43% more likely to report having received praise or recognition for their work in the last seven days

- 37% more likely to report that someone at work encourages their development

- 35% more likely to report coworker commitment to quality

- 28% more likely to report that in the last six months, someone at work has talked to them about their progress

- 27% more likely to report that the mission of their company makes them feel their job is important

- 27% more likely to report that their opinions seem to count at work

- 21% more likely to report that at work, they have the opportunity to do what they do best every day

This is one thing that hasn't changed over the years. So, if you aren't working to help build connections and friendships at work, you need to start. Agencies must facilitate opportunities for employees to connect personally, whether it be team lunches or team-building events like ax throwing, go-carts, golf, or bowling. You can also facilitate bonding with community service work involving the entire agency. Consider your culture and make sure the opportunities match your needs, wants, and expectations. If you plan a golf outing, and only a few employees are interested, it's a pointless activity. Many years ago, at a previous employer of mine, we talked a lot about potential team-building activities. Ultimately, we decided on softball, even though most of our team didn't even own gloves. We got players from each department to participate. Unlikely friendships arose out of this experience, and it provided a chance for team members to see me outside of the corporate environment.

Another friendship-building activity actually has a dual purpose. Forming work groups to solve problems within the agency historically provides great insights and a sense of unity when things go well. I suggest turning it into an out-of-office experience for a full day. If you keep them in the office for only an hour each time, too much focus is put on solving the problem instead of getting to know the others on a more personal level. There are countless ways to foster friendships. You just need to be deliberate and consistent.

Of course, despite your best efforts, there will likely be some teammates who still won't develop a friendship at the agency. If your agency is doing all the right things to facilitate friendships, and that one person hasn't engaged, it's a safe bet that they are highly negative, and that negativity is rubbing off on people. However, don't assume anything until you do some discovery.

Fifteen years ago, I had to pull an employee aside and have a serious talk about her relationship with her coworkers and how she felt they weren't including her. I had a compassionate but candid conversation about her verbalizing too much negativity regarding clients, processes, or even her personal life. I reminded her that she should come to me with any concerns or frustrations on the work front and shouldn't be venting about her personal issues in the office—at least not as frequently as it seemed to be happening. Long story short, she made some adjustments. Over the next few months, others noticed the change, and she was brought back into the fold. She was part of the group, grabbing lunches with them and joking around from that point on. These changes ultimately opened an opportunity for her to develop a deep friendship with an extremely positive coworker. When times got difficult for my past employer, and they had to make cuts, it put more work on the team. The two of them worked together to keep everyone who stayed unified and helped weather the storm.

Recognition

A recognition program helps build your culture and brand and should be a part of both your retention process and talent magnet. Recognition programs are a way to show employees your appreciation and that you value their contributions. There are several ways to show recognition, and you should match your program to your culture. The traditional areas for a program are achievements, behaviors, exceeding expectations, and milestones.

Think about it. How often are you recognizing your employees for their successes, and are you doing it in the way they receive best? Do you have any type of gift for anniversaries? What do you give to celebrate employees on their first anniversary? What about those who have been with you for five, ten, or twenty years?

What about top performers? Do you have an award for them?

What about other achievements or milestones? Did someone obtain a degree? Meet a customer satisfaction goal or revenue target? Maybe someone completed a number of hours of volunteer work or completed a big project outside of the office. What about years with the agency? Is there a carrot for continued loyalty to the agency that could make top performers think twice about leaving?

I have another favorite: an award for "Teammate of the Year." I recommend setting aside a decent bonus for this award. It should be voted on by team members, not management. Peers showing recognition will incentivize people to be helpful to others. It also creates a culture of gratitude, which is pretty much the antidote to negativity.

Whatever you choose to do, make it meaningful and buzzworthy. You want it to be desired and attainable by others. Most of your team members aren't getting celebrated elsewhere in life, so it's on us to help fill their tanks.

Flexibility for Life Events

Flexibility is a critical factor in employee retention. If we have learned anything from the pandemic, it's that employees need support when unexpected things happen in life. Parents had (and are still having) to make tough decisions about whether to quit their job because their kids had to stay home from school, do online learning, or home school. I may not pay the highest salaries (although I do compensate very well), but my staff attend all their kids' events and go to doctor appointments at the time of day that works best for them. I also don't subtract that from time worked.

Most of my competitors don't do that, which further helps my organization stand out when competing for talent and retaining employees.

Consider how you can be flexible and allow your employees to manage their time in ways that they see fit. Other cultures worldwide stay productive and profitable without dictating the clock and office presence.

Address Burnout

To follow along the lines of flexibility, as an agency owner, you must pay attention to the health and wellness of your team. Burnout happens to the best of us, even when working for an amazing organization. Further, the capacity of each person to avoid burnout is a moving target and depends on the individual. One person may have a higher tolerance than others. So, keep a finger on the pulse of your team.

There have been times when I told an employee to take a personal day to refresh (again, not counted as a vacation day) or brought in a chair massage. Please don't wait until it's too late.

When I see burnout, I ask what I can do to help. Employees will typically say nothing. That doesn't mean you're off the hook. Instead, dig deeper. I'll ask more than once or even suggest they go for a walk to take the pressure off. HR professionals will probably lose it over this, but I care more about my team's mental health than HR's standard operating procedures. In the end, they can tell I care far more about them as a person than as an employee, and for that, they are even more loyal.

Fun Perks

Go back and think about my example of Google and why it's considered a great place to work. You don't have to spend Google-level amounts of money to offer perks. For example, everyone in my office has a different beverage preference. As I mentioned earlier, I ensure my employees have their drinks of choice. In fact, we currently have six different types of sparkling water that we stock for them. Additionally, we find out their favorite snacks and ensure our kitchen is always stocked with them. These are small things, but they add up and show we listen, take notice, and care about our people.

Our office has taco Tuesdays and car washes every other week. These are nominal expenses but pay great dividends on the retention front. We did splurge for a golf simulator with kids' games as well. Team members can bring their kids after work or on weekends to play golf, kickball, homerun derby, and the like. It's unique, and word of our perks has definitely gotten around to recruiters.

My favorite is movie day. Get your team together in the conference room and whip out some classic '80s movies. I recommend *Willow* starring Val Kilmer. It's pure '80s gold.

The bottom line is that there's more to employee retention than pay. We must do a better job of listening, interacting, and showing we value our employees. When you do, you'll pull ahead of the competition in retaining current employees and attracting top talent.

But speaking of pay, it does need to be discussed. You should make it a habit to check with recruiters annually and make sure your compensation plan is at least in line with your competitors. If you're under market, you need to seriously think about adjusting. If you're doing most everything else right in the retention department, and you're in the wheelhouse of equal compensation, you really have little to fear from poaching. I strongly recommend you produce an annual statement of benefits and ultimate compensation so that each employee has a grasp of the cost the agency absorbs through their employment. Last, it's expressing to employees that there is only so much a given role can be paid that makes financial sense. Employees do best when given the truth about their trajectory, even if they don't like it.

CHAPTER 19:
AGENCIES DOING IT RIGHT

Perfection is not attainable. But if we chase perfection,
we can catch excellence.

—Vince Lombardi

One of the best things about successful people is that they're usually more than happy to share how they got there. And while they won't always give you a roadmap, per se, there are significant benefits to having someone provide you with practical advice on life "in the trenches."

In this chapter, we'll discuss some successful people and organizations in our industry that are doing things the right way. The goal? To inspire you to emulate their achievements by sharing some of their most valuable insights. And while you might not have the capital of a large firm, you're sure to find ways to implement their wisdom and practices into your own journey.

Jerry Conrey - Principal, Conrey Insurance Brokers

Jerry owns an agency that you might call "small to midsized." He was first licensed back in 1988 and went on to open his own firm, Conrey Insurance Brokers, in 2002. Currently, he has a team of ten located in Southern California.

Over the years, Jerry has cultivated a rather unique but very successful company culture. It is, first and foremost, performance driven. It also puts a lot of focus on the importance of knowledge. You see, Jerry subscribes to the belief that his employees have a career, not a job. As such, he does his best to provide them with both practical experience and educational opportunities. Since there's always room for improvement, he trades a traditional manager role for one that is mostly focused on mentorship.

What's most interesting is the way this philosophy carries over to his customer base. Rather than merely "sell" insurance, Jerry prefers to consult with his clients regarding products that either best suit their financial goals or resolve specific pain points. While this is typical for middle-market accounts, it's far rarer for small to medium accounts to receive that level of service. Instead of barraging them with sales pitches, he prefers to actually sit down with his customers and discuss their financial situations.

Jerry is a constant learner and is focused on improving himself first so that he can better serve others. He believes that as a leader, you should always reflect on what you're doing and maintain an awareness of your strengths and weaknesses. For example, he found that he could outservice his competitors by leveraging his team's education and financial knowledge, which had become deeply embedded in the office culture. Employees that were mentees would ultimately become mentors. On the other hand, he found that he was often getting in his own way by not delegating tasks and roles in a way that empowered his employees.

Though he's been in the industry long enough to be considered a veteran, Jerry has always maintained a growth mindset. It's easy to get comfortable with what you know and allow changes to lead to unwelcome frustration. However, he recognizes that change can also help weed out problems. In his opinion, the status quo is where the unproductive go to hide.

He confirmed this firsthand when he announced that his business would pivot toward a consultative approach. This change would also bring in a different type of client—one that valued a much more comprehensive risk management plan, which would naturally increase the workload on existing staff. Some team members took issue with the new philosophy, as it would not only change the status quo but also require an investment in education they were unwilling to make. Eventually, those who failed to adapt left. Those employees who shared and truly understood Jerry's vision for the agency invested in both themselves and others, which has led to greatly reduced turnover in their agency compared to their competitors.

Perhaps most importantly, Jerry didn't create his company culture to set a direction for only his employees. He actively lives it along with them. This all goes back to his mentorship mentality, something he embraces both in and out of the office. Moreover, a commitment to improving is evident in the systems and processes he's developed and his ongoing dedication to training and education.

As for his own shortcomings, Jerry quickly learned that he needed to delegate tasks and step away from things once in a while. In short, he needed to work *on* the business as opposed to *in* the business as much as he could—something quite difficult for an individual who's completely invested in the success of his clients. Once he adjusted, log jams were eliminated, and the change brought an opportunity for team members to grow into agency leaders. The time stepping away from the office has also created enough space to objectively look at performance and adjust tactics based on successes and failures.

Well ahead of the industry, Jerry started supporting a hybrid, work-from-home policy well before COVID-19 hit. He understood that results were far more important than presence in the office. He also understood team members' need for work-life balance and to take care of their families. This family-first focus has proved fruitful in attracting talent. Along with this change, he adjusted his recruiting efforts to look outside the industry and began to cultivate green candidates right out of college. This again was well ahead of his time. And while he does leverage professional recruiters, he rejects so-called resume pushers in favor of those who actively seek out talent.

Jerry also revamped his onboarding process and modified his HR practices to focus on cultural immersion. In fact, he connects with each new member of the team to better understand what was and was not attractive about their talent magnet. Additionally, when he was turned down by new talent, he'd interview them about why they said no and what he could do better.

The results?

Conrey Insurance Brokers has consistently maintained an annual growth in the double digits each year for the past decade and enjoys an extremely low turnover rate. When asked, Jerry is quick to attribute this success to having a hand on the pulse of his talent, ensuring each member of his team is properly aligned with the agency's values, culture, and client needs. All his efforts have made his agency a great talent magnet that holds its own against the larger agencies. Given this talent war, it speaks volumes.

Ofa Stead - Chief Human Resources Officer, Assured Partners

For our next success story, we're going to move into the billion-dollar agency arena.

Ofa Stead works for Assured Partners, the fifth largest privately held insurance agency in the country. This agency is scaling incredibly fast and continually needs a full talent pipeline to keep up. Her impressive resume includes over fifteen years in positions ranging from change management and human resources to leadership for both national and international firms. In her current role, she is tasked with solidifying AP's value proposition and strategies for talent acquisition and retention.

During our interview with Ofa, she was able to highlight what we might consider a common thread of organizational culture. In particular, she emphasized the need for kindness and a willingness to change with the tides to meet the needs of one's staff. She is a hands-on leader that prefers to listen, process, and propose solutions. Her first focus is to create solutions that provide immediate value for the organization while at the same time being mindful of the long-term challenges. As far as building a better talent magnet, she has prioritized identifying, improving, and communicating a clear value proposition for potential hires.

To illustrate, she used Goldman Sachs as an example. Of course, a firm of that size has a well-established reputation, and we can all imagine what it might be like to work there. From the outside, the culture might seem intimidating, even though we know getting a job at Goldman Sachs comes with prestige.

Looking at our industry, she asks an important question: "Why don't we, as agency owners, have a similar buzzworthy reputation or culture?" Ofa also stresses the need for agencies to tell both their origin story, where they are today, and where they are going. In short, agencies need to be promoting what it's like to work for our organization and then attract, train, and retain talent around the preestablished cultural narrative. Successfully communicating this on the front end will allow candidates to self-eliminate from the hiring process and serve as a confirmation to those aligned with the corporate values and vision.

About providing value to those that work for our agency, she stresses that agency culture needs to match the benefits offered. Ofa further explains that agencies will frequently listen to the needs of their team members but not take action that could improve the lives of their team. She is readily aware of this disconnect and the necessity to meet each generation's benefits needs where they are.

In fact, while most of us remain convinced that new hires will be satisfied with good pay and a flexible work schedule, remember that the top requested benefit by Millennials was pawternity leave, which came ahead of fertility expenses coverage, nap rooms, and free beer. Gym memberships didn't break the top twenty, and game rooms weren't in the top thirty. PTO and flexibility? They didn't even make the list!

In Ofa's opinion, offering a pick-and-mix benefits model would give current and potential employees the freedom to choose the options that best fit their needs while simultaneously making organizations far more competitive. She even suggests having something like flexible vouchers not rooted to base pay or bonus structure, such as a $1500 voucher option so that an employee who wants to bike to work can buy a bike. While firms would clearly need to set parameters around such options, benefit structures of this kind are something other companies simply aren't doing yet.

When asked about whether college degrees are necessary in today's workplace, Ofa maintains that degrees aren't essential if you can train in both technical and soft skills. According to her, what you can't teach or train is character. In a world where talent acquisition is no longer black and white, she added, degree requirements are a decidedly non-holistic approach.

In Ofa's opinion, talent goes through "Cycles of Consideration," which she describes as a process of give and take, during which both you and the candidate are thinking things over. This is where tools like LinkedIn and other social media outlets can make all the difference.

Ofa reinforced the importance of regularly scheduled events where candidates and employers can have meaningful conversations. If your agency will spend the money on events for prospects, why not invest in events that will bring talent to you and provide an opportunity to connect on a much more personal level?

While much of Ofa's wisdom is gleaned from large corporate processes, it's not hard to see how these concepts can be applied to smaller agencies—especially those that are eager to set themselves apart from the competition. At the very least, best practices like these can give us an indication of where things will be moving in the future and what is needed for smaller agencies to compete.

Rightsure and Lockton

Before we move on, I want to quickly discuss two agencies that are doing some things of note. The first is Rightsure Insurance Group, a medium-sized agency with two offices and fifty-two employees. The other is Lockton, which boasts more than 8,500 associates and 100 offices worldwide. Obviously, these two companies are different in many ways, but both have effective talent magnets.

Now, Rightsure has gotten a lot of attention since winning the Top Insurance Employer Award from Insurance Business Magazine in 2021. One of the areas in which they've really established themselves is maintaining a technology focus. In fact, they allow their employees an unprecedented amount of freedom and flexibility. As you can imagine, the fact that they were already letting their employees work from anywhere gave Rightsure a ton of agility when the pandemic hit.

Indeed, within a few months of the shutdown, they had already employed artificial intelligence in the form of chatbots to optimize their customer service. At the same time, they embraced a growth mindset that focused on continuing training and development for their employees. So, when the pandemic isolated everyone on their team, Rightsure was able to leverage its bond with its employees and minimize the impact on performance.

Then you have Lockton. This Kansas City–based firm is already known as one of the best places to work in the industry. As a matter of fact, they have been at the top or near the top of the list for over a decade now. Lockton takes a lot of care to highlight the fact that they are privately owned vs. publicly traded, which they believe gives the agency and its team members more freedom to meet client needs. By promoting training, development, and flexibility, they continue to attract top-quality talent eager to run their desks or book of business like their own "microbusiness." When you combine all this, you end up with a culture that is more akin to entrepreneurship than employment.

You don't necessarily need limitless capital and hundreds of staff members to facilitate the sort of changes that attract talent. Though each of the agencies we've discussed here is very different in size, resources, and capabilities, there are some common themes distinctly contributing to their success.

First, each of these agencies focuses on the importance of a defined culture. However, they also take the time to nurture talent so that it's in line with that culture. They also pay a lot of attention to employee needs, especially when those needs change. And though each has its own way of providing "flexibility" to their staff, they prioritize employee satisfaction and will do whatever it takes to maximize it. Last, all these agencies are committed to the development of their team members.

If you go back and compare the information in each chapter of this book to the agencies that are doing things the right way, you'd be hard-pressed to find a single discrepancy. Moreover, you should begin to realize that any agency, no matter the size, can build an effective talent magnet.

CHAPTER 20:
ROADMAP TO A SUCCESSFUL TALENT MAGNET

Invest in the future because that is where you are going to spend the rest of your life.

—Habeeb Akande

Some of you may have skipped all the way to the back of this book, looking for the action steps portion. I don't blame you. I tend to do that as well and then dig back into the book for details. So, let's sum this up in a simple (but again, admittedly difficult) step-by-step process:

1. **Change your mindset.** You have to reset and tell yourself and your staff that you're ready to learn, train, develop, and accept the challenge of building a twenty-first-century talent magnet. It starts with you. Your team won't go all in unless they see you burn your proverbial boat. The way you think things should be versus where they are and where they're going are likely not in sync. You must bring them into alignment if you're going to attract and retain the next generation of talent.

2. **Get a grasp on your current culture.** You need to understand the difference between the culture you believe exists and the one that does exist. The only way to do this is by asking your team members. Your team must have a tangible way to explain your culture to a prospective candidate, including its strengths and weaknesses.

3. **Develop a comprehensive and measurable diversity and inclusion strategy.** To survive, your workforce must look different tomorrow. To address the talent deficit, you'll need to look at areas that have previously been ignored and have a specific strategy to recruit them. But before that can happen, you must get your house in order.

4. **Do your opposition research.** Find out what the competition offers or doesn't offer. Is it pay and benefits, culture, advancement, or maybe a combination of all

three? If you're not providing a compelling offer for talent, you need to know why. Once you do, you must decide what you're going to do about it and whether you can even afford to do that. But the truth is, you can't afford to do nothing.

5. **Identify your future needs.** What people, systems, and processes are needed to achieve your agency's mission? Specifically, what roles might need to be created or eliminated? What skillsets are required going forward? What types of personalities would best serve to foster a healthy culture? Do you have a fully developed perpetuation plan?

6. **Identify and improve upon your existing value proposition.** This should evolve by identifying the benefits provided by competing agencies and adjustments made on your end. Don't forget to deliver on this value proposition for existing team members before advertising it to prospective hires. In short, be authentic. Walk the walk. Everyone in your organization must believe the value proposition is accurate and be able to effectively communicate it to others. This is more easily accomplished when implementing the retention strategies outlined in this book.

7. **Develop your recruitment strategy and build out your action plan.** Generate a roadmap for team members to follow with accountability checkpoints and specific measurable targets. You alone can't implement each strategy we talked about, so you'll need to identify in-office champions for this cause. Identify what you're

willing and not willing to do and the why behind it. Recognize the gaps and develop talking points to address them if they come up.

8. **Test, practice, review, and repeat.** You need existing staff to go through the candidate journey from start to finish, including interview roleplay. You might even consider a secret shopper of sorts to test the effectiveness of your process. Take the time to follow up with candidates that did not accept your offer and figure out whether there is anything else you could do differently the next time.

9. **Implement, analyze, and modify.** Implement your magnet, regularly assess what's working and what needs to change, then modify and repeat. You should never consider your talent magnet finished or complete.

The Bottom Line

The talent war isn't going away. As a matter of fact, it's only going to intensify due to the Great Resignation and employees aging out of the workforce. Many small- and medium-sized agencies are still behind in this realization and haven't fully committed to attracting top talent. If you made it this far, you're ahead of most.

Building a great talent magnet might seem like a monumental task. It is, but it's equally necessary. It's grow-or-die time. The future of your agency is dependent on the actions you take today. As a leader, you have an obligation to attract, hire, retain, and grow the next generation of insurance professionals. I promise, if you build the talent magnet, they will come.

APPENDIX

The following resources will help you manage your employees and will provide a template for the crucial points of every new hire's experience with your company.

From the interview to termination, these helpful sample guides will ensure that you are thorough, thoughtful, and prepared for every eventuality during your new hire's tenure with your agency.

Note: Feel free to adapt these resources to suit your agency's needs. For example, it may not be possible to ask all 50 questions in an interview. In fact, that would probably be overkill. Exercise your best judgement and do what suits your agency culture and style best.

50 INTERVIEW QUESTIONS

Try to prioritize five to ten of the questions below to ask all your candidates so that you can compare their answers. Asking all fifty questions would be overwhelming, so limit yourself to the ones that are most relevant to the position you are hiring for.

Some of these are meant to reveal personality, while some are meant to determine your candidates' motivations and aptitude for sales. Try to have a good mix of each so that you get a wide variety of information and a complete picture of the person you are interviewing.

50 INTERVIEW QUESTIONS

1. Why are you looking for a change?

2. How do you choose which listings you apply to?

3. Walk me through each of your roles, and something you learned or took away from each role.

4. Describe a mistake you have made, and how you resolved the situation.

5. Tell me about a time there was some tension with a coworker and yourself, and how you approached the situation.

6. If I were to call your current supervisor for a reference, what would they tell me?

7. What is one professional skill of yours that needs the most improvement?

8. What is your favorite task in your current role and why?

9. Which task do you like to complete the least in your current role and why?

10. What kind of opportunities are you looking for in this new role?

11. What kind of culture do you need to be successful?

12. What do you feel success would look like in this role for you?

13. How do you identify when you have too much on your

plate, and how do you address the issue?

14. What kind of management style allows you to thrive?

15. What drives you to get out of bed each day and bring your hustle?

16. I noticed you majored in XX and this position really does not relate to that topic. Do you plan to pursue opportunities in that field?

17. Tell me about a time you felt your idea was the best one but were instructed to do otherwise. How did you respond to that situation?

18. What do you expect in your first 30-90 days in this role if you were to be hired?

19. What do you think sets you apart from your peers and our other applicants?

20. Think of something you are passionate about, sell it to me.

21. If you were to be offered multiple opportunities, how would you decide which one to pursue?

22. If you have multiple projects on your plate at once, how do you decide what is the top priority?

23. Who are your role models and why?

24. Tell me about a time you were disappointed with your own work.

25. If you were CEO of the company you are working for currently, what is the first task you would execute?

26. Based on what you know about our company, what is one

thing you think could use improvement?

27. Define what servant leadership means to you.

28. What tactics do you utilize to motivate your teammates?

29. If you had to compare yourself to an animal, what would you be?

30. Before seeking this new opportunity, did you address the frustrations you have with your current manager? How did they respond? How could they have responded differently to influence your decision to stay with their company?

31. How many times have you brought your concerns to your manager in your current role? If they were not being addressed properly, did you try any other routes or approaches to resolve the issues?

32. What are your worries, and why?

33. Tell me why our company sounds better than the company you are with currently, and better than others you have seen while you have been applying?

34. What is the title of the last book you read and the one you are reading now?

35. What role do you play in your group of friends?

36. Tell me about an area in which you are truly an expert.

37. Had you remained at your current employer, what was your end goal there?

38. Tell me about a time you set difficult goals for yourself

and how you achieved them.

39. Have you ever set difficult goals for your team? How did you ensure they met them without burnout?

40. What is something you have done professionally that you would not want to repeat?

41. Define what hard work looks like to you.

42. Would you rather be late, but perfect? Or on time, but only good?

43. In 5 minutes or less, can you explain something complex to me simply, as if I were 5 years old?

44. If I were to hand you $50,000 to start a business, how would you use the money?

45. How many of your coworkers would say they are a fan of yours?

46. What is the best interview question you have ever been asked, and why?

47. How would you sell hot chocolate in Florida in the dead of summer?

48. Choose between being the #1 employee with all of your peers disliking you and being #15, but everyone liking you.

49. What do you think people would say about you at your funeral?

50. Name a song that describes your work ethic.

BEST PRACTICES FOR YOUR NEW EMPLOYEE'S FIRST DAY

It is really important to set the right tone for your new hires from the very beginning. By doing a little prep work before they arrive, you'll make a great first impression on them and increase the chance of them staying on with your company long term.

Follow the steps below to ensure that you are preparing both your company and your new hire for their first day of working together as a team. If some of these steps do not apply, feel free to skip them. There are some items that may apply to remote workers as well as in-office positions, but most of these are created with an in-office position in mind.

Use this example as a jumping off point to create and adapt a version for remote work if you need it.

BEST PRACTICES FOR YOUR NEW EMPLOYEE'S FIRST DAY

1. Make sure they know what to bring on their first day:
    a. Driver's License
    b. Social Security Card, Passport, or Birth Certificate
    c. Banking Info for Direct Deposit
    d. Anything job specific (ie; closed toed shoes, their own laptop, etc.)

2. Be sure they have contact information for who they should connect with on arrival (in case of emergency) and any lingering questions.

3. Be sure they know where to park and what to wear.

4. Make sure their desk is clean and free of any unnecessary items.

5. Be sure their phone is clean, working and cleared of any prior employee's greetings.

6. Be sure their computer has been cleaned up of all items on the desktop, reset their background, history and cache are cleared, unnecessary bookmarks are removed.

7. Clean and sanitize their mouse and keyboard.

8. Make sure drawers to their desk have been fully emptied.

9. Make sure they have all essentials (pens, pencils, stapler, tape, etc.).

10. If their email is set up, go ahead and sign them in.

11. Create logins for every platform they need to access ahead of time, and bookmark them on their browsers.

12. Give them a small notebook filled with their logins and passwords for everything.

13. Provide a list of all your employees' names, emails, and extensions (or the most relevant people, depending on the size of your operation).

14. If a uniform is required, ask their size ahead of time and have them ready and waiting.

15. Have their business cards ready to go on their desk.

16. Have your team sign a welcome card that is on their desk waiting for them.

17. Have all benefit options ready in a folder for them to take home and review.

18. Take them to lunch on their first day and get to know a bit about their interests outside of work.

19. Be sure they know where everything is (copier, extra office supplies, break room, bathroom, how to obtain extra uniforms if needed, etc.).

20. Send out a welcome email after lunch with a photo and 3 facts about that person to the entire team. This gives your other employees conversation topics to connect with them on and makes the new hire feel a bit more welcomed.

NEW HIRE ONBOARDING ASSIGNMENT

When your new hire starts working with you, it can be helpful to give them a worksheet to set expectations and give them a clear goal for their first interactions with your company. Have your new hires complete this worksheet within the first week of their job and make sure they are set up for success.

There is also an intro paragraph on the worksheet to help explain to your new hires why you are asking them to complete this. This is a key point that should be carried through their tenure at your agency, explaining why. By providing valid reasons for the things that you ask your employees to do, they will have more buy-in, greater understanding of the goals you are trying to accomplish, and a clearer vision of what their role and expectations are to help meet them.

NEW HIRE ONBOARDING ASSIGNMENT

As a new team member at our agency, we believe it is critical that you learn and understand our performance expectations, key priorities, resources, and the agency information you need to perform in your role. This assignment is to be completed at the end of your onboarding process. Please talk with your teammates if you feel you are missing any of the information needed to complete this assignment. Once completed, you will review this document with your manager which will ensure that we are all on the same page from the start.

Key Job Responsibilities:

What are the most critical responsibilities of this position?

☐

☐

☐

☐

☐

Key Expectations:

What specific and measurable tasks must I complete within my first 60 to 90 days?

☐

☐

☐

☐

☐

Interactions:

Who are the key people with whom I will work with on a daily/weekly basis?

NAME	TITLE	THEIR ROLE

EMPLOYEE EVALUATION WORKSHEET

The following worksheet is intended for employees to fill out at the time of their review. There is a section for them to self-evaluate, as well as a section to evaluate their managers.

Try to give the employees ample time to fill out this sheet before the actual review meeting so that they can think through their answers.

Don't forget to dedicate time in their review meeting to go over the results in this worksheet. There's nothing worse for your employee than putting effort and thought into this evaluation, only for it to be glanced at briefly and ignored.

Self-Evaluation

I demonstrated	when I
I successfully completed	and, it resulted in
I think my communication style with management is	
I think the quality of work I produce is	
I think the quantity of work I produce is	
I think my attitude is	

I think I am open to new ideas and new ways of doings things:	☐ Yes	No
I think I take constructive feedback well:	☐ Yes	No
I think I work well with my teammates:	☐ Yes	No

I recognize	could use improvement. I plan to work on it by

Additional Comments:

Evaluation of Manager by Employee

I feel comfortable communicating my concerns with my manager:	☐ Yes	☐ No
If no, what would make you feel safer to do so:		
Do you feel you have enough guidance on tasks and projects:	☐ Yes	☐ No
Do you feel you are given feedback often enough:	☐ Yes	☐ No
I would love to learn	to be more successful.	
I feel motivated to come to work:	☐ Yes	☐ No
If no, what can be done to improve this for you?		
I feel my ideas are welcomed and thoughtfully considered:	☐ Yes	☐ No
If no, please explain further:		

Additional Comments:

Employee Signature:	Date:
Management Signature:	Date:

LEADERSHIP QUESTIONNAIRE

Have your employees fill out the following questionnaire to evaluate leadership at your agency. You can have them evaluate leadership as a whole, or their own direct manager specifically. Note areas for improvement and note areas of excellence. Make sure this survey is anonymous so you can get honest answers from your employees.

Also, if you would like to go over the results with the team, be sure to keep an open mind about your need to improve. This is the time to eat some of that humble pie I have mentioned previously. You are asking them for honest feedback, and the way you respond to that will determine their comfort level with doing so in the future.

LEADERSHIP QUESTIONNAIRE

Rate the following skills from 1-5.

People Skills

- How effective are they at connecting and relating with employees?
- How effective are they at building rapport and maintaining relationships with clients?
- How effective are they at resolving employee conflicts?
- How effective are they at navigating difficult conversations with clients?

Communication Skills

- How effective are they at listening to and understanding employee concerns?
- How effective are they at listening to and understanding client concerns?
- How effective are their verbal communications skills?
- How effective are their written communication skills?

Problem Solving Skills

- How effective are they in resolving complex challenges for clients?
- How effective are they in negotiating favorable solutions for clients?

Execution Skills

- How effective are they at following through on commitments to the team?
- How effective are they at responding to your requests for assistance?

Leadership Skills

- How effective are they at motivating employees to perform well?
- How effective are they at training employees?
- How effective are they at showing empathy for employee challenges?
- How effective are they in leading weekly agency meetings?

Management Skills

- How effective are they at communicating the vision for the agency?
- How effective are they at defining job roles within the agency?
- How effective are they at holding employees accountable for their actions?

Coverage Knowledge

- How well does he/she understand the coverage challenges for your clients?
- How committed are they to developing coverage knowledge within the agency?

EXIT INTERVIEW

When an employee leaves your company of their own volition, you will want to ask them for feedback so that you can get a clear understanding of what can be improved and why this person is leaving. You may assume you know the reasons why, but the truth may be different from what you perceive it to be so you should always ask.

Your employee may not feel comfortable answering these questions unless you explain that you are just trying to figure out ways to make your company a better place to work. By framing it as them helping you to improve, they are less likely to feel as though they are being investigated for wrongdoing.

Also, at this point you should assume that it is too late to try and retain your employee, so approach this conversation as a learning opportunity and nothing more. The time to try and retain someone is when they first approach you about leaving and provide their notice.

Just like a candidate interview, asking all 20 questions may be overwhelming, so pick and choose the ones that you feel most strongly about to ask first. If you have a good relationship with your employee, they may be receptive to continuing through all the questions, but you should start with the most crucial ones and stop when you sense the person is no longer offering any further useful information.

EXIT INTERVIEW

1. How long ago did you begin looking for another opportunity?

2. What drove you to look elsewhere?

3. What portion of your new offer is most appealing that we do not offer?

4. Have you brought your concerns up to anyone here?

    a. If yes, how many times and to whom? Also, how long before looking for a new opportunity did you begin voicing these concerns?

    b. If no, why not? Did you not feel safe or comfortable? What could we have done differently to have allowed you the room to speak up?

5. Would ever consider employment with us in the future and why or why not?

6. What would you have needed to remain an employee here happily?

7. Do you feel you had all the tools necessary to complete your job to the standard we held you to?

8. Could you please describe the culture you feel we have created here?

9. Did you feel like a valued member here, why or why not?

10. Do you feel your responsibilities remained the same

throughout your employment, and if they changed, do you feel you were communicated to about that change clearly?

11. What was your favorite and least favorite part of your role here?

12. If you were CEO, what is one change you would make to improve morale?

13. Tell me about one skill you feel we strengthened for you and one we could have helped you with.

14. Describe your best day working here, and your worst day working here.

15. If you were able to redesign your role here, what would you change?

16. Would you recommend this company to a friend that is looking for a change? Why or why not?

17. What is your advice for improving our training and development process?

18. Were you given feedback on your performance overall?

19. Were you given guidance and direction to achieve your goals?

20. What is one valuable piece of information or lesson you will take away from your time here?

TERMINATION CHECKLIST

The following checklist should cover all the basic items you need to complete whenever an employee leaves your company, whether voluntarily or not. It can be adapted/adjusted to suit your agency's preferred procedures. Ensuring that all of these items are checked off will allow a smooth transition out of your agency for both your remaining staff as well as the person leaving.

While some of these items may not apply, the checklist is intended to get you to think about these fine details. You may find that while you don't need to collect an iPad from your terminated employee, you do need to collect some other specialized equipment that was on loan from your agency, and that seeing the list jogs that memory.

TERMINATION CHECKLIST

Employee Name:

Supervisor:

Forwarding Address (if Applicable):

Best Contact Number:

Last Date Worked:

Last Date Paid Through:

Termination Due to:

_____ Voluntary Resignation with Written Confirmation

_____ Termination Of Employment Via Employer

      _____ Explanation Given to Employee

      _____ HR Has Reviewed Employee File

      _____ Signed Letter of Termination Provided to Employee

_____ Other (Military, Death, Etc.) _____ Reason
_____ Supporting Documentation Received

_____ Final Wages Reviewed with Employee

_____ Check To Be Direct Deposited: _____ Acct #
_____Routing # _____ Bank

_____ Check To Be Picked Up by Employee

_____ Check To Be Picked Up by Persons Authorized by
Employee

Authorized Person's Name _____

_____ Check To Be Mailed

Address To Mail _____

Hours Of Benefit Pay to Be Paid Out _____

Rehire Eligible: Y / N

Discussion Of Potential References: Y / N

Subsequent Access to Premises: Y / N

Collect From Employee:

_____ Fob

_____ Closest/Locker/Vehicle/Office Keys

_____ Final Timesheet Fully Completed

_____ Work Cell Phone

_____ iPad

_____ Laptop

_____ Parking Tag

_____ ID Card

_____ Training Manuals

_____ Any Additional Proprietary Materials

Cancel:

_____ Work Email

_____ Computer Access

_____ Benefits

_____ Direct Deposit

_____ Remove from Phone List

_____ Forward/Cancel Extension

For Employee:

_____ COBRA Information

_____ HR Contact Info

_____ Exit Interview

_____ Personal Belongings Removed from Workspace

_____ Clean Work Area

Notes: _____

Signature of Supervisor and Date:

_____

EXCERPT FROM "AGENCY AMPLIFIED"

The following chapter is an excerpt from Justin's previous book, "Agency Amplified: Achieving Scale in a Shifting Digital Landscape," now available for purchase on Amazon.

THE TALENT ASSESSMENT BLUEPRINT

The rising use of technology in the hiring process by employers and applicants has significantly lowered the entry barrier for job seekers. A single job posting can now generate hundreds of applicants, leaving agency leaders and HR departments a wealth of choices—perhaps too many. Rather than having too few applicants, many agencies now must comb through a stack (or inbox full) of resumes to find the right candidate.

Separating the good candidates from the bad can be a frustrating, time-consuming process that prohibits employers from carefully reviewing applications. Studies show that most applicants spend less than two minutes reading the job description. Consequently, many applicants often fail to meet the minimum requirements for a job. As the need to weed out these applications grows, HR departments need ways to efficiently differentiate a good application from a bad one—otherwise, bad applicants may make their way to the interview stage while more-qualified candidates are erroneously passed over.

The best agencies know how to make a fully informed decision about whether a candidate is a good or bad hire. They know the solutions available to streamline the hiring process. By utilizing better preemployment technology, agencies can save themselves time, money, and a lot of exhaustive effort.

In this chapter, I talk about what preemployment tests are, what they do, the benefits they provide to agencies and their potential new hires, and how to best use preemployment tests to bring about optimal results.

What Are Preemployment Tests?

Preemployment tests are tools an employer can use to collect pertinent data from potential hires in an objective and standardized way. Quality tests are created by professionals, reviewed thoroughly, and provide an efficient and effective way for employers to prescreen applicants for critical capabilities and traits. A preemployment test may even provide insight into the level of productivity to expect from a potential new hire.

There is a wide selection of preemployment tests available, but most tests will fall into three categories:

1. Aptitude
2. Personality
3. Skills

Let's take a moment to look at the purpose of each of these three tests.

Aptitude Tests

Aptitude tests measure critical thinking, problem-solving skills, and the ability to learn, retain, and apply new information. In short, aptitude tests assess an applicant's overall intelligence and brainpower.

Problem-solving skills and the ability to learn and apply new information are particularly critical in the insurance industry. Finding talent that possesses both qualities is a win-win for the employee and the agency's long-term success.

Personality Tests

Personality tests have gained popularity in many companies, but there is still a lot of confusion about what these types of tests measure and how to use them.

At their core, personality tests provide insight into these questions:

1. Will the candidate be comfortable in this role?

2. Does the candidate possess the character and behavioral traits that will lead to success in this role?

The personality test can assess whether a candidate has a behavioral inclination that fits both the position and the agency's culture. There are numerous options as far as the traits that can be measure by this type of test, but most tests follow a five-factor model that evaluates agreeableness, conscientiousness, extroversion, openness, and stress tolerance. These five factors are becoming increasingly popular over the traditional introvert-extrovert, type A–Type B models.

Using a five-factor model gives a broader, more in-depth look at aspects of personalities that paint a better picture of a candidate's fit in a particular role. Effective personality tests can also reduce turnover since they can uncover whether a candidate would be happy and comfortable working in a specific job.

To illustrate this last point, let's look at two roles that exist in every agency: sales and service.

A salesperson is generally going to be assertive and competitive. A service person, on the other hand, needs to be cooperative and patient.

By utilizing the personality test in the hiring process, an agency can identify a match (or mismatch) based on general required personality traits for the role versus those traits the applicant possesses.

Skills Tests

A skills test helps measure specific capabilities needed for the job, such as a candidate's ability to complete an Association for Cooperative Operations Research and Development (ACORD) form. Skills tests can also evaluate insurance knowledge; verbal, math, and communication skills; and typing and computer proficiency.

Candidates may have picked up these skills in school or prior work experience, but they may not always be featured on a resume or be on par with their aptitude. Therefore, a skills test is a great way to assess whether an applicant knows enough to complete the job effectively.

How Can Agencies Benefit from Using Preemployment Tests?

Prescreening employees via tests offers agencies the opportunity streamline the hiring process so it meets their needs. Some agencies may only use tests for certain roles, and others may find great benefits in using preemployment tests uniformly across the organization. Here are some of the improvements to the hiring process that agencies should expect to see.

Time Savings

While there will certainly be serious and qualified applicants for a job, a significant percentage of applicants will need to be filtered out. Whether a job posting generates fifty applicants or over two hundred applicants, that's still a lot of resumes to sift through, even to do just a quick review for red flags. Any person who has spent time in this type of process can attest that the breaking point is just after the first twenty-five resumes.

By adding a preemployment test at the beginning of the process, agencies can quickly eliminate candidates who are not qualified. Agencies will save significant time (and headache) reviewing resumes and reduce the time spent interviewing unqualified applicants. This extra time and energy can then go toward evaluating serious candidates.

Cost Savings

The saying "time is money" applies to the painstaking hiring process. There is a cost associated with every step of recruiting, from the expense of advertising for an open position to the salaries of every person involved in interviewing, extending and negotiating offers, onboarding, and training. The cost of the turnover and the need to reinitiate the hiring cycle further compounds hiring expenses.

The use of preemployment testing narrows the field of candidates at the top of the funnel, meaning fewer resumes require a full review. Even fewer candidates make on to the interview stage. Preemployment testing also provides increased assurance that the right candidate with the right qualifications, aptitude, and personality will be hired, reducing concerns about overall turnover. Both byproducts represent significant cost savings to an agency at all stages of the hiring process.

Less Guesswork

Data continues to be vital to knowing and understanding clients in the insurance industry, but data can also play a crucial role when looking to bring new talent into an organization. Without data, hiring decisions happen based on experience and intuition. While both certainly serve a purpose, relying on preemployment tests helps by providing objective data based on job-specific criteria. Utilizing data removes a significant portion of the guesswork and allows agency leaders to make more-informed decisions.

A Clear Picture of Employee Productivity

It can be hard to judge how effective a job candidate will be based solely on their resume and interview chops. The applicant's goal, after all, is to paint themselves in their best light—but the painting doesn't always match reality.

Preemployment tests can predict a candidates' potential productivity by assessing whether the applicant has the right knowledge, skills, and abilities to perform as expected.

A More Objective Standard

Preemployment tests adhere to federal guidelines, which encourage more equitable and nondiscriminatory hiring processes.

This high level of regulation helps companies maintain a more objective selection process. Generally, tests are less subjective and help reduce bias that can otherwise become an issue during the hiring process.

A well-validated test will not evaluate age, sex, race, or any other criteria that can lead to a suit about unfair hiring practices. As long as tests are created based on job-related skills and traits, a test can provide better defensibility should a suit be brought against the agency.

Implementing Preemployment Testing

Preemployment tests are not an out-of-the-box solution. They require some build-out for the agency to significantly benefit from adding tests to their current hiring process.

Here are the steps that are most critical to making preemployment testing a success.

1. Job Analysis. Each role in the agency will need to be reviewed and evaluated to create a thorough job description, which includes the skills, work activities, and abilities required for the job. Based on this information, the selection of test criteria can measure the specific skills, abilities, and personality traits that produce optimal performance in the role.

2. Decide on Test Relevancy. After a job is analyzed, leaders can then decide what tests are most pertinent. Perhaps one role requires skills and aptitude tests but not a personality test. Other roles may need all three to assess candidate capabilities accurately. The goal should be to decide which tests best suit the needs of the role and helps agency leaders make the most informed decision while hiring.

3. Decide When to Test. Testing early in the hiring process can prevent extra work down the line. It allows hiring managers to collect objective data about candidates and ensure that anyone who makes it to the next stage meets the position's basic skill requirements. Early testing can save significant time and effort that would typically be required to evaluate an overwhelming number of resumes.

There is no wrong answer; it is more a question of consistency and the desired outcome.

4. Establish Protocol for Remote Testing. Most likely, candidates are not coming to the office to complete the preemployment test, especially if testing is being required early in the process. Creating written guidelines about how to take the test will help prevent confusion and reduce the candidate's potential for fraudulent activity.

5. Test Existing Employees. Administering tests to current employees will help the agency establish scoring guidelines for each role and associated test. While you may be tempted to only test top-performers, it is crucial to test employees of all levels. A broader selection of employee scores can help you to establish more appropriate benchmarking levels for future hires. As a bonus, testing current employees also allows managers to assess current staff and better understand pain points or areas where employees excel.

6. Establish Scoring Guidelines. Based on the ranges provided in testing employees in step 5, agency leaders will need to decide on a minimum and maximum acceptable score for each role and associated preemployment test. Scores that are too low can be a reliable indicator of turnover due to poor performance, while scores that are too high can indicate that an employee will be bored or restless and may leave on their own in search of something more challenging.

Additional Evaluation

Preemployment tests can provide significant advantages to agencies during the hiring process, but it is essential to remember that there is no guaranteed solution to avoiding bad hires. An employee may score high and perform poorly, and a candidate that scores low could still be a top performer in the agency.

There is no magic bullet, and agencies must continue to do their due diligence by consistently evaluating the same criteria for applicants, including resumes, interviews, prior experience, education, and any other factors that may be relevant to the role. Preemployment tests are a significant first step and complement the process of reviewing resumes and conducting interviews, but agencies need to maintain realistic expectations, and use tests to improve, not replace, current hiring practices.

Nonetheless, implementing testing can take a substantial amount of friction out of a challenging process by giving agency leaders insight to make more efficient and effective hiring decisions.